Heidegger's *Being and Time*

Indiana Philosophical Guides

Titles in the series include:
Kant's *Critique of Pure Reason*
Douglas Burnham with Harvey Young

Derrida's *Of Grammatology*
Arthur Bradley

Heidegger's *Being and Time*
William Large

Forthcoming:
Descartes' *Meditations on First Philosophy*
Kurt Brandhorst

Husserl's *The Crisis of European Sciences and Transcendental Phenomenology*
Katrin Joost

Plato's *Republic*
Darren Sheppard

Spinoza's *Ethics*
Beth Lord

Heidegger's *Being and Time*

William Large

Indiana University Press
Bloomington and Indianapolis

This book is a publication of

Indiana University Press
601 North Morton Street
Bloomington, Indiana 47404-3797 USA

http://iupress.indiana.edu

Telephone orders	800-842-6796
Fax orders	812-855-7931
Orders by e-mail	iuporder@indiana.edu

The paper used in this publication meets the minimum requirements of American National
Standard for Information Sciences—Permanence of Paper for Printed Library Materials,
ANSI Z39.48-1984.

Typeset in 11/13 pt. Monotype Baskerville by
Servis Filmsetting Ltd., Manchester

Manufactured in Great Britain

Cataloging information is available from the Library of Congress.

ISBN 978-0-253-35264-4 (cl.)
ISBN 978-0-253-22036-3 (pbk.)

1 2 3 4 5 13 12 11 10 09 08

Contents

Series Editor's Preface   vii
Acknowledgments   ix
Abbreviations   xi

Introduction   1

1. **Historical Context**   3
   From Phenomenology to Ontology   3

2. **A Guide to the Text**   19
   The Question of Being   19
   Being-in-the-World   34
   Others, Language and Truth   51
   Anxiety, Death and Guilt   66
   Time and History   83

3. **Study Aids**   105
   Glossary   105
   Further Reading   127
   Works by Heidegger   128
   Recommended Secondary Works on *Being and Time*   134
   Other Works Cited   138
   Writing an Essay on Heidegger's *Being and Time*   139

Index   147

Series Editor's Preface

To us, the principle of this series of books is clear and simple: what readers new to philosophical classics need first and foremost is help with *reading* these key texts. That is to say, help with the often antique or artificial style, the twists and turns of arguments on the page, as well as the vocabulary found in many philosophical works. New readers also need help with those first few daunting and disorienting sections of these books, the point of which are not at all obvious. The books in this series take you through each text step-by-step, explaining complex key terms and difficult passages which help to illustrate the way a philosopher thinks in prose.

We have designed each volume in the series to correspond to the way the texts are actually taught at universities around the world, and have included helpful guidance on writing university-level essays or examination answers. Designed to be read alongside the text, our aim is to enable you to *read* philosophical texts with confidence and perception. This will enable you to make your own judgements on the texts, and on the variety of opinions to be found concerning them. We want you to feel able to join the great dialogue of philosophy, rather than remain a well-informed eavesdropper.

Douglas Burnham

Acknowledgments

The writing of this book was supported by a research grant from the University College Plymouth, St Mark and St John, for which I am very grateful. I would also like to thank the series editor Douglas Burnham and Carol Macdonald the commissioning editor from Edinburgh University Press for their patience and helpful advice. Finally I would like to thank my friends and colleagues who read different versions of this manuscript: Arthur Bradley, Paul Bentley, Rob Brown, Lars Iyer, Meredith Millar, Val Reardon, Paul Sutton and David Webb.

Abbreviations

There are two English translations of *Being and Time*. One, by Macquarrie and Robinson (Oxford: Basil Blackwell, 1962), and the other by Stambaugh (Albany: State University of New York Press, 1996). I shall be using the first translation with the abbreviation BT throughout.

Introduction

No commentary can hope to substitute for the reading of the text itself, but it can provide a helping hand. *Being and Time* is probably one of the most important books written in the twentieth century. It has influenced not only philosophers, but a wide range of people from writers and poets to psychiatrists and scientists. Like Kant's *Critique of Pure Reason*, it announces a fundamental shift in the way we understand ourselves and the world, and we are perhaps still wrestling today with all its ramifications and consequences. This book is meant only to provide assistance for the student and the general reader and does not engage in any detailed way with the scholarship surrounding this work (which the reader might imagine is quite vast).

Unlike the other commentaries on *Being and Time*, however, it does come from a different background. Nearly all the introductory books in English on this work are heavily influenced by Dreyfus' great work *Being-in-the-World*. There are probably two reasons for this: firstly, one of the great strengths of this book is that it tries to explain Heidegger rather than just imitate him; and secondly, it springs from the analytic tradition (at least the 'soft' kind of Wittgenstein, Austin and Searle) which is dominant both in the US and the UK. There is nothing wrong with this, but it does tend to ignore the manner in which the book was first received, in France, and I believe has quite a different way of reading Heidegger which does not so much focus on epistemological questions (even if they are always overturned in relation to ontology) and the first division of *Being and Time*. This present book comes from a serious engagement with the French Heideggerians for many years, and I have indicated what some of the debates are within this reception in the end notes to the chapters. Still it is meant to be only a guide and I keep most of the material out of the main text and simply explain Heidegger's argument as well as I can. It gives this book, I believe, a different flavour and style from the other commentaries on *Being and Time*.

Many introductions to *Being and Time* begin with a paragraph listing significant dates in Heidegger's biography (when he was born, went to university and died). I think these are a waste of time in the modern world where the Web can provide information about everyone in an instant. More importantly, however, I do not think any of these facts can tell us anything at all about the meaning and importance of a philosophy, however titillating they may be. None the less, there is one important exception in the case of Heidegger and that is his involvement with the Nazi party. There has been a furore about this matter throughout the academic community and across the world. The details of Heidegger's complicity can be found in any serious biography (and I refer to Safranski's *Martin Heidegger: Between Good and Evil* in the text), but what is more significant is if it should stop us reading and teaching his work and if it infects his philosophy as a whole. To the first, I would say 'no', because for the very reasons above, I do not think we should conflate the meaning of text with the author's life. To the second, however, I would say, 'yes', because I maintain what is lacking in *Being and Time*, and perhaps all of Heidegger's work, is a serious engagement with ethics. No one more than the French philosopher Emmanuel Levinas has shown us how important this absence is. Such a topic is well beyond the scope of a guide, but I have indicated its seriousness in some of the end notes to the chapters.

This book is organised in three parts: introduction and historical context; commentary; and study aids. The general reader may wish to skip the last part, although the glossary and further reading may be useful.

1. Historical Context

From Phenomenology to Ontology

Heidegger famously began a lecture series on Aristotle with this statement: 'He was born at such and such a time, he worked and he died.'[1] Such is true of all philosophers. What is important about them, their only serious achievement, is their philosophy. Everything else is quite meaningless and trivial. Nothing about their lives tells us anything significant about their philosophy. The only way to understand the beginning of a philosophy is to understand how it begins itself; that is to say, philosophically. *Being and Time* begins with the question of Being, but it does so almost as though there were no context, as though it had dropped from the heavens. I believe that to make sense of this question, we first of all have to begin with its method, how and why it is asked.

This method is phenomenology. It is not my ambition, here, to explain it completely. All we need to do is to understand its basic principles (how is it different from other ways of doing philosophy, for example) and how Heidegger himself understood this method and applied it to *Being and Time*. This introduction is, therefore, divided into three parts. The first describes very briefly and succinctly Husserl's explanation of phenomenology (Husserl was Heidegger's teacher and inventor of this method). The second, what Heidegger thought (even though he was to use this method in all his philosophical work) was deficient in Husserl's application of phenomenology. And finally, the third, how specifically Heidegger illustrates and puts into practice this method in *Being and Time*. Once we have done this work we will be ready to begin the actual first pages of the book itself in the next chapter.

Edmund Husserl and the Phenomenological Method

No one should underestimate the influence of Husserl on Heidegger, both personally and intellectually. Indeed, it is not possible at all to understand one word of *Being and Time* unless one has at least some grasp of the phenomenological method. Luckily for us we do not need to understand the whole of this movement, but only what is relevant to our own reading, and we give here only the briefest of explanations, since this is all we need for our purposes. What is at the heart of phenomenology is first of all a refusal of metaphysics and academic philosophy. This is the meaning of the famous slogan of the phenomenologists 'Back to the things themselves!' This is not just a method of doing philosophy, but also an attitude of mind. Throughout the history of philosophy, there are moments when it grinds to a dead halt; becomes ossified and lifeless. What matters at these times is not that one is doing philosophy but rather that one knows a lot about philosophy. Doing and knowing about philosophy, however, are very different things. You can know a lot about Plato, Aristotle and Kant, for example, but be unable to utter a single philosophical sentence. When Husserl told his students that they should get back to the things themselves, what he meant was that he was not interested in what they knew about philosophy, what they had learnt at school or university, but whether they could talk philosophically about what they saw – the table in front of them, for example.

'What do I see?' This seems a very simple question, but the more I think about it the more complex and difficult it becomes (especially when I am not allowed to be clever by referring to anything I have read but only to describe what I see). This phenomenological attitude is very important to take into our reading of *Being and Time*. For all the difficulty and jargon (which has more to do with the translation, than the German itself) of this book, what matters to Heidegger is our everyday experience of the world. Unfortunately what is closest to us is also what is hardest to see precisely because of what we have learnt at school and university, whether consciously or not, which acts as a screen between the world and ourselves and distorts our experience.

For Husserl, what I discover when I look at things is that what determines my relation to them is an 'intention'. There is no doubt intentionality is not new to phenomenology. Husserl borrowed the expression from his teacher Brentano, and he probably took it from the Scholastics. But it is not enough to know this, as we said above, for no amount of reading books tells me about my experience. What I have to do is to apply it to what I see. I have to ask myself not 'Where does this word come from?', as though this was doing philosophy, but 'Does this word help me understand what I am seeing?'

What, then, is Husserl trying to get at by using this word? Simply put, what he is saying is that when I look at something, let us say a tree, I do not just see something, but always see it *as* something: never the tree, but always the tree as a tree. We shall see later that this phenomenological 'as', becomes very important to *Being and Time* in explaining how we relate to the world generally.[2] Contained in this 'as' is the meaning of Husserl's intentionality. First of all, we have to stop thinking of consciousness as an empty sack which in some mysterious way I take out into the world and fill with my experience of things. For Husserl, on the contrary, and experience teaches us this, consciousness is already outside of itself, already related to things in the world from the very beginning.[3] The world is not something out there, rather we are our world.

This idea that consciousness is already outside of itself in the world, Husserl explains as 'consciousness of . . .'. There is no such thing as 'consciousness', if one understands this word to refer to some kind of mysterious thing like the 'I' or the self, rather there is only a relation. Consciousness is always consciousness of something, never just consciousness. Try it for yourself. Try and perceive without perceiving something, or think without thinking something, or imagine without imagining something. There can be no consciousness without consciousness of something, and it does not matter whether this 'something' is real or not. I can have a consciousness of a unicorn, for example, without there being a real unicorn. What is important are not claims about reality (a metaphysical problem, not a phenomenological one), but how consciousness experiences the world, and how in relating to things these exist now as something perceived, now as something imagined, now as something useful, and so on. There is not a subject and object separate from one another, which then, through some kind of unexplainable and unknowable process, have to become linked or attached. Rather, they are already intertwined in our direct experience of the world. This is what is meant by 'consciousness' when we no longer think of it as a philosophical word, but as our experience of the world.

We are not interested in Husserl, however, for his own sake, but for his impact, great as it was, on the young Heidegger. Here our guide can be a set of lectures which were the first draft of *Being and Time*, and which were published after his death. These lectures are called the *History of the Concept of Time* and they are by far the best introduction and context to this work not only because they are its immediate origin, but also (as many of his students testify) because Heidegger was a remarkable teacher and presented his thought in the most direct and vivid way in his classes.[4]

The History of the Concept of Time

The first two chapters of the *History of the Concept of Time* follow our description of the phenomenology, but in greater detail than we need for our first reading of *Being and Time*. They also provide the first version of Heidegger's explanation of the word 'phenomenology', which he puts forward for the second time in the book itself, and which we will look at in the next section. What specifically interests us at this moment, however, is Heidegger's break with some aspects of Husserl's phenomenology in the third chapter of the *History of the Concept of Time*, which is a kind of immanent critique. The difference between them will explain to us more clearly the specific nature of phenomenology that underpins *Being and Time*, as opposed to its general definition.

Heidegger tells us, in the opening pages of this chapter, that what has been left unquestioned in phenomenology till now is the question of Being. This does not mean that the question is not present and that we require a completely different method in order to uncover it. Rather, phenomenology presupposes it, and for this reason is the only method we can hope will answer it. This way into the question of Being is quite different from the opening of *Being and Time*, which is historical in nature, in the sense of a history of philosophy. None the less Heidegger's criticism of the traditional way of asking the question of Being already presupposes this phenomenological approach.

We need to leave aside, at the moment, just how *Being and Time* opens, and also what exactly the question of Being might be.[5] This might appear quite strange, because usually when we think about what a question is we are convinced the right way to approach it is through its answer. Thus, I understand the question of Being, if I know what is asked about in this question, which would be, in this case, the meaning of Being itself.

Philosophical questions, however, are quite different; for if I knew the answer to this question, why would I bother asking it in the first place? Heidegger's problem is that we think we know the answer only because we are asking the question in the wrong way. The problem of the question of Being, therefore, at least at first, is not to know the answer, but how to ask the question correctly in the first place. This is why we have to go through the detour of understanding phenomenology first, before we can even begin to read *Being and Time*, otherwise our expectations will already destroy the possibility of us getting anything worthwhile from our reading. We might think, for example, that a true understanding of Being is to supply its definition, and we might wonder why Heidegger does not do so; or, as Heidegger suggests at the start of the book, that it is not a serious question at all because everyone knows the answer already.

What, then, are Heidegger's problems with phenomenology as it is traditionally conceived? When it first began, it restricted itself to the problems of logic and epistemology. In other words, how can I know objects in the world and that I am making true statements about them? It saw this relation primarily in scientific terms. As I have already remarked, the key notion of phenomenology is intentionality, but what concerns Heidegger here is the kind of consciousness it presumes. Not what is intentionality, but how does intentionality, as a certain kind of behaviour or conduct, come about. We can speak about chairs and tables, and the structures of perception and judgement which make our shared experience of them possible, but what Heidegger wants us to ask is why or how we relate to things like this initially. Who or what are we such that we relate to the world intentionally? It is this question of Being which is presupposed by traditional phenomenology but is left unquestioned. Is this question not more fundamental than intentionality (understood in the restricted sense), for if we did not relate to the world in this way, then there would be no meaning of things at all to think about? Meaning is not in the things themselves but in the way we speak and talk about or even judge them.

Heidegger claims Husserl's first answer to this question is what he calls the 'natural attitude', and in this attitude I think of myself like any other object in the world, such as trees, houses and cars. I am as 'real' as they are. The main thrust of phenomenology, however, is to show that I am not the same as other things. One way in which I am different is that I not only relate to things in the world (I am conscious of them in a way they are not conscious of me), but can also relate to this relation. I not only perceive the table, but also reflect upon myself perceiving the table. The difference between the two relations is that in the latter the object is immanent to reflection, whereas in the former it is transcendent. When I think about something I perceive, then the object must be internal to the thinking itself, whereas it is quite obvious that the chair I perceive is external. Thus, what is truly mine is only what I am conscious of as part of my consciousness, and the 'material world,' as Heidegger writes, 'is alien and other', even though as a real human being, I must belong to it.[6] I, as a concrete living thing, seem to be part of nature, but at the same time, as conscious, absolutely separate from it.

The supreme paradox of phenomenology, Heidegger argues, is that this absolute split between myself and the world is the very condition of objectivity. For it arises not from the transcendent perception (the external world), but the immanent reflection on this perception (thought). If there were only transcendent perceptions, then there would be no objectivity at all. I would experience this tree, then that one and so on. The concept 'tree', which unifies my experience, comes from my side of the reflection on perception, which is internal to consciousness, and not from the transcendence of the world.

The performance of the phenomenology reduction, Heidegger explains, is when I focus my attention not on the object of perception itself (my involvement with it in the real world) but on the act of perceiving as it is reflected upon, and only in this way is the objectivity of the object of perception given to me. This is what Husserl means when he says that we must 'bracket the world' in order to reflect upon what we are doing when we perceive something. I say 'I see a tree' and the 'I' and the 'tree' belong to the real world. But if I think about it, this is not what I am doing at all. What in fact is going on is that I am thinking about the act of perceiving as something immanent to reflection, and not the object perceived as external. When I now think about the object in this act of perception (which has become part of my reflection), then it too has become immanent, and Heidegger tells us this is where all phenomenological analysis begins. He is keen to underline that this does not mean the rejection of the object, but a change of our orientation towards it: how it appears to us through our perceiving it, rather than what it is in the natural attitude.[7]

The tree is not part of my consciousness. It is something 'alien' and 'other', but the tree as immanent to the act of reflection on my perception is. Thus, we can distinguish between the tree as 'real' (external to consciousness) and as 'objective' (internal to consciousness). If it is internal to consciousness, then it must have the same Being as consciousness, and then, Heidegger adds, it must be 'absolutely given'. The real tree can change. I go to the park, and it is no longer there, but if I reflect upon my perception of that tree it must be absolutely present in it. It would be absurd to say it does not exist in this way, even if the material world has changed. How Husserl envisions phenomenology, therefore, (and which makes his method very similar to Descartes) is that there must be an absolute split between the world and consciousness. But how is this division, Heidegger asks, possible, when the very beings for whom this separation occurs (ourselves as concrete living beings) also belong to the world?

The Being of that being which is consciousness is taken for granted by the traditional method of phenomenology, and yet without it, it could not function at all. But why should we, first of all, be thought of in terms of consciousness? Does this way of relating to the world sum up who or what we are, and is it the only way in which we relate to the world? It is not only that traditional phenomenology does not have any answers to these questions, but it does not even ask them. It takes it for granted that we are nothing but 'consciousness', and being conscious is to be directly understood through intentionality as objectivity. It does not ask about this because it fails to follow its own maxim, 'Back to the things themselves'. It finds the Being of things in the world in the objectivity of consciousness, but it does not investigate the Being of consciousness with the same rigour. Rather than being true to the Being of consciousness (in the way in which it has been true to the Being of things, describing how and what appears), it has imported a metaphysical meaning of consciousness from the history of philosophy (essentially Cartesian).

What is important for Heidegger is not the definition of the structure of intentionality as such, but the Being of that being who relates to the world intentionally. In other words, you and I, as real, existing, individuals, and not as abstract poles of a relation of knowledge in which we speak of tables and chairs in philosophy lectures or books. Even though Husserl, like Descartes and Kant, understands the Being of the object through the subject, its Being is in fact only interpreted through this relation and not as it appears in itself. The subject vanishes in the very objectivity of knowledge, and just as the real chair is purified of any material being, so too is the consciousness which intentionally relates to it. Knowledge takes precedence over the terms in the relation, and they both evaporate in its abstraction. This is why Husserl's notion of consciousness can in fact tell us nothing about that being which is conscious (ourselves as concrete living beings). Our lives have completely disappeared in thought, and there is no way of getting back to them through this way of doing phenomenology.

When we come to our reading of *Being and Time*, we shall see that Husserl's understanding of consciousness is in fact general to the history of philosophy as a whole. It takes knowledge to be the primary way of relating to the world, and understands consciousness through this relation. Heidegger's orientation is quite different. He asks who that being which is conscious is and should we take its way of relating to itself and the world primarily to be one of knowledge? Is there not a more fundamental and practical way of engaging with the world from which this objective relation is in fact derived? This rejection of the letter of Husserl's phenomenology, however, is not a repudiation of its spirit, for we can only get back to this more elemental meaning of our lives (which has disappeared in the history of philosophy because of its obsession with knowledge) by being true to our own experience of ourselves and the world. Heidegger's method in *Being and Time*, then, could be described as a double reduction. It seeks to get behind what Husserl's reduction takes for granted, the life of the individual consciousness, and thereby uncover a more fundamental ontological basis to any possible epistemology, which cannot, in its turn, be reduced to an abstraction of thought. For though it might make sense to claim that the objectivity of the chair is only ideal, and its factual existence does not matter in order for it to be thought, it is absurd also to claim that the existence of the person who thinks this thought is of no concern for them or others.

For Heidegger, Husserl's phenomenology goes astray not because of the reduction, but because of its conception of the natural attitude, which is anything but natural. This is because it is not sufficiently philosophical enough. It takes what is a commonplace point of view to be a philosophical truth without sufficiently questioning whether it is or not. It assumes we first of all encounter things in the world as what Heidegger calls 'objectively on hand' and we ourselves also belong to this same relation.[8] Is it true to say we experience ourselves as merely one more natural object in a world of natural objects? There is no doubt, in a restricted sense, we can. So for example, when I am ill, the doctor treats my symptoms and not myself (though we can imagine a good doctor would do both). But even here we can see the difference between a mere thing and a human being. For we all know the difference between a disease and being healthy. The first is merely biological, whereas the second involves the whole of someone's life, such that two people could have the same illness, the one being healthy and the other not. The natural attitude, rather than being natural is something we have actively to decide to have. It is not, except for philosophers, the ordinary way in which human beings experience the world, but only a possible one and not the most fundamental.

It might seem a long detour to read these pages of the *History of the Concept of Time* before we go on to *Being and Time* itself, but they are important to understanding what is at stake in the latter. First of all, and most importantly, we must realise it is a work of phenomenology. Heidegger's way into the question of Being is phenomenological. We can grasp this in two ways: first, it is impossible fully to comprehend this work without any knowledge of the influence and impact of Husserl's method on Heidegger's thought; but also secondly (and perhaps more importantly), he takes further what Husserl has given him by laying bare its hidden ontology. It is through this critique that Heidegger discovers his own ontology. Beyond the relationship between Heidegger and Husserl, however, this immanent critique of phenomenology also explains the opening of *Being and Time*. For although, as we shall see in the next chapter, it begins with the question of Being, this question can only be approached through the question of what it means to be a human being. The reason why Husserl did not, or could not, ask what it meant to be a human being, or could only understand it in a restricted way, is that he himself did not have a sufficient understanding of Being. The question of Being and the different but related question of what it means to be a human being are, therefore, inextricably bound together.[9]

Phenomenology in *Being and Time*

It is not until the seventh section of the introduction of *Being and Time* that Heidegger actually explains what he understands phenomenology to be. It is clear from reading this section it is not merely a historical curiosity, but a real and essential way of doing philosophy. Indeed, for Heidegger, it is the only way in which the question of Being is going to be reawakened and possibly revealed to us. As a method, if it is properly practised, it is true to the phenomena themselves, and allows us, therefore, to escape the distorting vision of tradition, which, as we have just seen, even affected the way Husserl understood, or failed to understand, consciousness.

This is why Heidegger can say, in the *History of the Concept of Time*, that Husserl's phenomenology, properly speaking, is 'unphenomenological', even though Husserl himself invented this method, because he is still caught up within a dominant tradition of philosophy which is essentially Cartesian.[10] As we shall see, this is not a stupid error on Husserl's part, as though if he were only cleverer he might have broken out of this prejudice, but it belongs to the very Being of human beings that we are always captured and enslaved by our past. Indeed, such indebtedness to the past is one important way we are very different from other beings in the world. Our past is not external to our present, but belongs intimately to it. We live the past through the present, and the present through the past.[11]

Phenomenology must first of all be understood as a method and this is what distinguishes it from theology, sociology or biology, whose modes of inquiry are determined by what they study (God, society or life), rather than how they investigate their subject matter (BT: 58–9). As I have already stated, Heidegger understands this method through the famous slogan 'Back to the things themselves'. This gives us the first clue (perhaps the most important) to his definition of phenomenology. It is a descriptive philosophy which attempts to describe how things appear without placing upon them extraneous matter. Here, Heidegger is no different from Husserl, who writes in his *Ideas* the following important maxim:

Throughout phenomenology one must have the courage to accept what is really to be seen in the phenomenon precisely as it presents itself rather than interpreting it away, and honestly describe it. All theories must be directed accordingly.[12]

Where they part company is that Husserl takes it as obvious that it is simple to begin in this way but just ends up repeating the very metaphysics phenomenology was meant not to presuppose. In Heidegger's terms, he does just 'interpret away' the phenomenon.

We cannot turn our backs on the past, but we can uncover possibilities within it which have been buried by the majority point of view. We have forgotten 'what is really to be seen', because we already interpret it through a given theory. But there must have been a time when people really did see things as they were and their words described what they saw.[13] For us such a people were the ancient Greeks, whose words contain their original experience of the world, and form the basis of our philosophical vocabulary (although these have become stale and hackneyed through thoughtless repetition). This is not a question of etymology for the sake of it; or even of discovering the 'truth' about the Greeks, as though we could experience their world in exactly the same way as they did; for we can only have access to the past from our present, even though this past shapes and determines it. Rather, by coming to these words again, trying to understand them on their own terms, we can win back our own experience of 'what is really to be seen'. This also explains the peculiar nature of Heidegger's etymologies. His aim is not to be correct, as in a dictionary definition, but to make us think again and not accept our tradition naively.

When we come to Heidegger's etymology of the word 'phenomenology', he reminds us that it is made of two Greek words: 'phenomenon' and 'logos' (in Greek, *phainomenon* and *logos*) (BT: 58). Why he specifically wants us to go back to the Greek is in order to dislodge us from understanding 'phenomenon' as appearance, where the word (in the Kantian tradition) means an object of consciousness, as opposed to the thing in itself: the tree as it appears to me, rather than what it really is. In some interpretations of Kant, the relation between the appearance and the 'thing in itself' (or in the Kantian vocabulary, the noumenon) is causal. The 'thing in itself' is the mysterious cause of what we see, but we ourselves can only experience it through our kind of consciousness (for Kant, a combination of the categories of the understanding, and the pure forms of intuition, time and space). Heidegger uses the analogy of an illness to describe the same causal understanding of appearance (BT: 52). My temperature is merely a symptom or indication of an illness which is in fact hidden.

Such an understanding of phenomenon as appearance is merely derivative. For the notion of 'hiddenness' or 'being concealed' is dependent first of all on there being something visible. What is present is 'indicated' in what shows itself. There must be something visible before I can make a judgement about it as mere appearance or symptom. This is what we discover when we go back to the original etymological meaning of the word. For 'phenomenon' derives from the present middle infinitive *phainesthai*, 'to show itself' or 'to bring itself to light'.[14] The word 'phenomenon' should be translated, therefore, as 'that which shows itself in itself', and not first of all as 'appearance'. Phenomena, therefore, are those things which can be brought into the light, which the Greeks called 'beings' (*ta onta*). This meaning of the word 'phenomenon' is more primordial and original than the definition of appearance as an 'object of consciousness'. In other words, there are only objects of consciousness because first of all there are visible things in the light of the day, and not the other way around.

If the other half of the Greek etymology of phenomenology is *logos*, then the proper meaning of this word has been concealed in the history of philosophy. It is interpreted as 'positing', or 'judging', and thus as 'reason', 'judgement', 'conceptuality', 'definition', 'ground' or 'relation' (BT: 55).[15] In both cases, we need to return to a more fundamental experience of things which has been covered over by our metaphysics; not by deducing the meaning of experience from our theoretical categories, but by digging deeper into our everyday lives and finding what is already there. Only a truly descriptive phenomenology can actually break out of this metaphysical tradition.

If *logos* does not mean all these above definitions, then what does it mean? It is not primarily to be understood as judgement, but as a 'making clear' (*Offenbarmachen*) of something (BT: 56). Here we can see that the etymology of two stems of 'phenomenology' are very close, since 'phenomenon', as we have just seen, means 'manifestation' (*Offenbare*). To speak about something is to make that thing present, to 'bring it to light', as we might say in English, and the logical forms of judgement are not original but dependent on this first 'making something clear'. To speak the truth about something, in the original Greek meaning of the word, is not first of all to assert a true judgement, as opposed to a false one, but to make it clear what we are talking about, so that some judgement could be made about it. It is to bring to light, when we speak to one another, what was in the dark, so that the listener can grasp what is being talking about.

This notion of 'unconcealment', Heidegger argues, is a literal translation of the Greek word for truth, *aletheia*, which will be central to his re-interpretation of 'truth' later in *Being and Time* (BT: 256–73).[16] It is also an important gauge of how we are to take what Heidegger himself writes in *Being and Time*. What is written here is not argued for, if we understand 'arguing' as derived from some principle of logic. On the contrary, it is revealed or made visible. It appeals to readers' own experience of themselves and their world. Its status as 'true' is whether it shows our experience in a new light so that we can grasp it in a more radical manner. Perhaps some people's exasperation in reading Heidegger is that they want a logical argument rather than a description. For Heidegger, logical arguments are always derivative and never the place to begin a philosophical investigation.

In combining these two etymological definitions, Heidegger can arrive at an initial conception of phenomenology as follows: 'To let that which shows itself be seen from itself in the very way in which it shows itself from itself' (BT: 58). This should not be confused with naiveté. Just because we do not import a theory from the outside in order to understand the phenomena before us, does not mean they are just lying there simply to be investigated. On the contrary, they are always concealed from us, and this is precisely why phenomenology is required. But what is it that remains hidden? Heidegger's answer is their Being. In terms of our own reading of *Being and Time*, we do not know, at this stage, what this question of Being means, but what is sought here already tells us how Heidegger will fashion his own phenomenology.

Every phenomenology is ontology. It looks to the meaning of the Being of phenomena. This meaning is hidden, but we should not take this to imply that it lies somewhere else or exists behind things, as in the Kantian definition of appearance. It shows itself, so to speak, in their 'showing', but rather than being simply available and present to us, we have to look for it. Heidegger also tells us at the end of this section, and again we will have to wait till the next chapter for a full explanation of why this is so, that there is one being whose Being is crucial to this investigation, and this is ourselves, or what Heidegger calls in German, *Dasein*, which most translators leave untranslated (BT: 61–2).

Why are we more significant than any other being? Because we are the only beings for whom the question of Being can be a question at all. Stones, trees and lizards do not ask what it means to be, only ourselves. Thus, our being will be the way into the question of Being in general. Heidegger calls this method 'fundamental ontology', and the specific interpretation of Dasein 'the analytic of the existentiality of existence' (BT: 62). All of this will become clearer to us as we go on, but he leaves us one last tantalising, yet very important and decisive clue to the overall argument of *Being and Time* (and why some have been critical of fundamental ontology as a whole) as to how he will pursue *Dasein*'s Being.[17]

He writes at the beginning of *Being and Time* that Being should not be thought through the categories of genus or class, as has been traditionally the case (as though Being were the mere definition of something) but rather is something higher which he calls '*transcendens*' (BT: 22). More specifically, the transcendence of Dasein lies in its 'radical individuation' (BT: 62). What makes Dasein different from any other being, and allows it to be our way into the question of Being, is that it, amongst all other beings, can be an individual. We will have to wait to see what this 'being an individual' means as we go through this book, and how it differs from what we might ordinarily understand from this expression.

Notes

1. As reported by Kisiel in *The Genesis of Heidegger's* Being and Time (1993: 287).
2. Heidegger makes a distinction between the 'as' of assertion and the 'as' of interpretation in s. 33 (BT: 195–203). His argument is that I already have to understand the world before I can make judgements about things in the world. I discuss this difference in 3, 'Moods, Understanding and Language', pp. 56–63.

3. Heidegger will repeat this manoeuvre in *Being and Time*, when he criticises the Cartesian explanation of the world, which places us externally to a world we already exist within (BT: 122–34). I discuss Heidegger's critique of Descartes in detail in 'Descartes and Space', pp. 46–51.

4. Gadamer (one of Heidegger's most important students) writes a wonderful testimony of the effect of his teaching on his students. See Gadamer 1994: 61–7.

5. I discuss this in the section 'From Beings to Being' on, pp. 20–6.

6. *History of the Concept of Time* (1985), p. 97.

7. This reduction can go through a further step, which is called the eidectic reduction, where I now no longer focus on my own individual acts (my perceiving this tree at 3 o'clock in the afternoon, for instance) but what is true in every act of perceiving, judging or imagining, and so on.

8. *History of the Concept of Time*, p. 111. 'Objectively on hand', becomes 'present-to-hand' in *Being and Time*, which I will explain in the section 'The World', pp. 39–46.

9. In fact, *Being and Time* is a preliminary work, since it deals with the Being of human beings only as clue to the meaning of Being in general and not Being as such.

10. *History of the Concept of Time*, p. 128.

11. Heidegger calls this relation to the past 'thrownness' (*Geworfenheit*) (BT: 219–24). To free ourselves from the past is not to disown it, but to make its possibilities our own. I shall discuss this relation between the past and history in the section 'History', pp. 94–7.

12. Husserl 1982: 257.

13. There is a double appeal in *Being and Time*. One is to experience and the other to history which preserves the truth of this experience. We no longer have a direct access to the truth of this experience (though we, so to speak, experience it every day), because of a fateful decision within this history which means we have lost this truth. We therefore need to reclaim it for ourselves. This is the purpose of *Being and Time*, and also explains Heidegger's invocation to a time before the 'fall' (the Pre-Socratics), marginalia with the dominant history of Western thought, other ways of the thinking (the 'East') and speaking of the truth (poetry in the broadest sense of the word), after its publication.

14. The verb is the middle form of *phainō*, which means 'to bring to light', whose stem, according to Heidegger, is *pha-* from which the Greek word for light or daylight, *phōs*, also derives.

15. In fact, the interpretation of phenomenon as appearance goes hand in hand with this translation, for objects of consciousness are things about which I make judgements, and for Kant their existence is deduced from such judgements. See Kant 2003: 104–99.

16. I shall examine the important of Heidegger's notion of truth in the section, 'Truth and Reality', pp. 63–6.

17. I am thinking especially of Levinas here, who would argue this emphasis on the self in *Being and Time* seriously distorts our ethical relation to others. For his early critique of Heidegger, see his essay, 'Is Ontology Fundamental?'.

2. A Guide to the Text

The Question of Being

Let us now look at the rest of the introduction of *Being and Time* having understood and grasped the importance of the phenomenological method to its overall argument. Introductions are always the most difficult to comprehend in any book, because they already presuppose that we know what is being investigated. Here the author informs us what the book is about, but we as readers might be entirely in the dark, so much so that we might not even understand why the book was written in the first place. Secondly, it is in the introduction that the author will lay on the table, for the first time, the tools through which the investigation will proceed. In philosophy, this is usually the technical vocabulary with which any research is possible. The difficulty of making sense of these words is only further compounded if the author is attempting to make an original contribution, for then they are likely to have to invent new words in order that we can see the problem in a original way, rather than relying on our learned knowledge, or even ignorance. Of course, it is up to us as readers to decide if this originality is worth it or not. Both these issues are visible in the introduction to *Being and Time*. First of all, we are not at all sure what Heidegger means by the question of Being, and even whether it is worthwhile, and secondly he will throw into these first pages a lot of special terminology which we will never have encountered before. It is no surprise, therefore, that many readers never get beyond these first few pages, or will complain that Heidegger is an unnecessarily difficult and impenetrable writer.

Having said this, however, philosophy, even though it might always push at the limits of language, is always about the simplest matters.

Unfortunately what is simple can be the most difficult to understand. For Heidegger, the question of Being is not a technical question which only the cleverest people can ask who have had many years of training in philosophy. On the contrary, we all already have an under-standing of Being, even if we do not know how to put it into words. In this chapter, we will examine in detail the rest of the introduction to *Being and Time* (we only looked at the section on phenomenology in the introduction) and it is divided into three sections. The first explains why Heidegger thinks the question of Being has been for-gotten and what the difference between beings and Being is (even if the latter can only be done in the most perfunctory and incomplete way, since this difference is the very problem of Heidegger's thought and not only in *Being and Time*). The second investigates why, in rela-tion to the question of Being (as I ended in the introduction) Dasein has a fundamental priority for Heidegger, and why also, as we shall see in the third section, this necessitates what he calls the 'destruction of the history of ontology'. Finally, we will conclude with what the overall aim of *Being and Time* as a whole is, and how the structure of the book reflects Heidegger's intentions, or even fails to do so.

From Beings to Being

Heidegger, in the opening pages of *Being and Time*, wants us to feel the very strangeness and peculiarity of the question of Being. Like the stranger in Plato's *Sophist*, which he quotes in the exergue, we thought we knew what this question meant, but now we are no longer sure (BT: 1). Our position is doubly difficult. Not only do we not know the answer to the question, we do not even know how to ask the question properly or even what the question is asking us. There are good his-torical reasons, which we shall come to in the third section of this chapter, why we are so perplexed, but we must all start with some understanding of Being, otherwise there would be nowhere to begin at all. It is just that our own presuppositions and assumptions get in the way of us seeing what is there before us.

Let us then start with our ordinary understanding of Being and see if this helps to get us beyond our initial confusion. All of us already use Being in our ordinary conversations. I say, 'The sky is very blue today.' Already in this little word 'is', I imply a meaning of Being, even if, were someone to ask, I would not be able to define it. I suppose if

I were going to make a stab at it, I would say 'is' means 'exists', and if I were going to give a very tortuous reply, I would say, 'The sky is very blue today' means 'There is something which is the sky that exists which is very blue today.' But already in my explanation, which I know is very clumsy, there are two meanings of Being. One is the thing itself which I am talking about, the sky, and the other is the very fact of its existence. In German, this distinction is easy to make linguistically because it can be expressed by the grammatical difference between 'being' (*Seiende*), meaning a being, and 'Being' (*Sein*), meaning existence. Already from the translation of these two words, we can see a problem: in English, we use the same word 'being' to describe the two different meanings. This is why most translators of Heidegger (as we have already been doing so far in this book) write 'Being' with a capital to mean existence, and 'being' with a small 'b' to mean something which exists.

Of course, there are many kinds of beings. A stone is a being, a mathematical formula is a being, and even you and I are beings. What is common to all these beings is that they exist – they 'are' in some way. Obviously, they are not all in the same way. I am not in the same way that a stone is (or even an animal, Heidegger will say in a lecture he gave after he wrote *Being and Time*),[1] and quite clearly I am not in the same way that a mathematical formula is. None the less, and this is what is so strange and peculiar about the question of Being, even though all these beings are in a different way we all agree that they are. What does the word 'Being' mean such that I can use it of everything and yet it does really seem to say anything at all since it does not pick out any specific character of a being, like the property red or hard might do?

That there is not an easy and readily available answer to this question is not just because it is hard to answer, but also that the tradition handed down to us (which even has the name 'ontology') makes it virtually impossible for us to do so. We do need, however, to be careful here. It is not that Heidegger just wants to damn the whole of our past. In fact he makes it clear that the question of Being is not 'new' at all, but rather a very ancient question (BT: 40). His relation to the past is ambivalent. On the one hand, it prevents us from understanding the question of Being, but on the other, the only resources for renewing this question come from this past. What allows us to tease open what is genuine in the past is always our own present experience of Being. The past is of no interest for Heidegger, if we mean by it simply facts and information about a bygone age. What counts is whether the past reveals to us who we are (why we are not the same as a stone, or a mathematical formula).

There is no doubt it is Aristotle more than any other philosopher who determines Heidegger's approach to the question of Being. We might say that he has the same ambiguous relationship to him as we all have to the past. On the one hand, Aristotle is the first philosopher to take the question of Being seriously as the fundamental question, and also there is no doubt that even the later analysis of Dasein is shaped by Heidegger's reading of Aristotle's *Nicomachean Ethics*.[2] On the other hand, however, it is Aristotle's setting out of the question of Being that has led to its being forgotten and neglected. This is why Heidegger can write of Aristotle that he 'put the problem of Being on what was, in principle, a new basis' (BT: 22), but at the same time *Being and Time* is aimed at overthrowing Aristotle's conception of time as an adequate understanding of Being (BT: 48).[3]

How, then, does Aristotle understand Being? The key here is comprehending what he means by definition, and why the meaning of Being is so problematic in relation to it. In Aristotle's vocabulary, I define something by first knowing what genus it belongs to and then what species within this genus. Thus, 'man' belongs to the genus 'animal', and then by picking out what differentiates it from any other species in the genus, rationality, I can arrive at the definition, 'rational animal'. Even Aristotle realised that such a process could not be used to explain the meaning of Being, because there is no specific difference which you could point to that would distinguish it from anything else (remember our initial discussion that I can say I am, a mathematical formula is, the sky is, and so on). As Magda King writes, I can explain the genus 'animal' by pointing to a horse, but it would be strange to point to a horse and say, 'This is what I mean by "is".'[4] How would you know what I was pointing at to determine Being's meaning? Its eyes, ears, legs, colour?

The reason why Being transcends every genus is that it is common to every being, but because the only way in which it can define things is by picking out specific differences, there does not seem to be any way in which to say anything about Being. Although we might all be happy to say that everything is, 'is' itself does not seem to have any properties or attributes. Now for Heidegger this is an important clue, since it precisely shows us that Being and beings are not the same because we cannot use the same language to speak about them. In terms of the history of philosophy, however, the transcendence of Being merely proves it is 'the most universal and emptiest of concepts (BT: 2).

So, from Aristotle's way of understanding Being, we end up with the idea it is indefinable, but this conclusion is only a result of us thinking Being must be defined in exactly the same way as beings. Perhaps it is the classical form of definition which is inappropriate rather than that Being has no meaning, and is so unsuitable that some will even wind up saying the opposite. Not that Being is indefinable, but it is the most self-evident of concepts. Did not I just say that we use the meaning of Being in the most ordinary and everyday expression, such as 'The sky is blue' and 'I am happy', so why do we need to take it seriously as a philosophical problem?

Such sentences only demonstrate what the ordinary understanding of Being is. We cannot conclude from them that Being is meaningless. Our difficulty just shows us there is a puzzle here, even in our everyday relation to the world. We already have an understanding of Being, since everyone knows what these ordinary sentences mean, and yet at the same time we cannot say precisely what this meaning is. Philosophy dismisses this ordinary understanding of Being, because philosophy rejects our everyday lives. To be a philosopher is to reject the ordinary world and the opinions of the 'every man'. As we shall see, through our reading of *Being and Time*, this disapproval has to do with a particular bias in Western philosophy towards theoretical knowledge. It is just such a tendency which has led to the meaning of Being falling into perplexity. For Heidegger, therefore, it is exactly within our ordinary understanding of our relation to the world where we will find the clues for reawakening the question of Being: 'The very fact that we already live in an understanding of Being and that the meaning of Being is still veiled in darkness proves that it is necessary in principle to raise this question again' (BT: 23).

Before we can begin to ask this question, however, we first must know what it is to ask a question at all. Perhaps we have a tendency, when asking questions, immediately to jump to the answer, and if we cannot find it, then we assume the question is not a serious one. What Heidegger wants us to do is to slow down (always important when you are doing philosophy). He wants us to ask ourselves what does it mean to ask a question, any question whatsoever, even if this question does not have an answer. This is important for two reasons. Generally, if we barge through questions without adequately thinking about what the question is asking us, then it is very likely we will come out with the wrong answer. Secondly, and more importantly, thinking about the question might actually give us a clue how we might go about questioning itself. Remember *Being and Time* begins with a question. In fact, you could argue that the aim of this book is solely to reawaken this question (so that we might take it seriously again) and not to answer it (so if you think philosophy is about answers rather than questions, you might end up being disappointed).

Every question, Heidegger tells us, and not just the question of Being, can be broken down into three main elements:[5]

1. What is asked about – *das Gefragtes*
2. What is interrogated – *das Befragtes*
3. What is discovered by asking this question – *das Erfragtes*. (BT: 24)

How can we apply this list to Heidegger's own question? What we are asking about is the meaning of Being, but in order to ask this question we need to interrogate a specific kind of being. Even though we already have a pre-understanding of Being, we cannot just ask directly about the meaning of Being, because, as we have already discovered, in reading the first pages of the introduction, we end up having nothing to say at all. The only access to the meaning of Being is through beings. The further question, then, faces us: what being? As I sit at my table writing this chapter, I am surrounded by many kinds of beings: the light which shines on the papers I am reading, the pile of books I am using to try to understand *Being and Time*, the pencil with which I am writing my notes, to name but a few. Can I pick one of these in order to begin my investigation? There is one important being, however, I have intentionally left out of my list, and that is myself, for I too am a being. We already know from the last sentences of our introduction that the kind of being I am has a certain importance and significance for Heidegger. Before we get to why this is so, let us ask about the other beings, and why they cannot be a route into the question of the meaning of Being.

Heidegger's formal answer to why not is that his question has an 'ontological priority' (BT: 28). When I ask questions about the kind of beings I have given as examples, then what I am doing is asking what they are (in Heidegger's vocabulary, he calls these ontical questions, so as to distinguish them from ontological ones). The most sophisticated kind of questions in this fashion are scientific. If I really want to know what a pencil is, then I should ask a scientist, and not a philosopher. We live in a culture, perhaps, which tends to think the only important questions are scientific, but when it comes to the question of the meaning of Being, science has nothing to say. Negatively, we have already seen why this must be so, because if we take a scientific attitude (or a philosophical one which is largely inspired by it), then we cannot say anything about the meaning of Being at all. On its own, however, this does not really mean much, because this could just as equally be a proof that it is not really a proper question at all and we should just stay silent. Heidegger has to give us a positive reason why we should carry on with this question.

His first response is a very Husserlian (or even Kantian) one. All the sciences, no matter what they are, are 'regional ontologies' (BT: 10). What he means by this is that they each, in their own turn, investigate a specific region or type of being. Thus, mathematics investigates mathematical objects; physics, physical ones; history, historical ones, and so on.[6] What none of these sciences studies is the meaning of Being as such, for if they did they would no longer be the disciplines they were, but something quite different, namely philosophy. This does not mean that the sciences do not have an ontology, but it is simply presupposed in order that scientists can get on with their work. The physicist, for example, does not worry about whether the universe she is describing exists or not, but is merely concerned with whether her interpretation of the facts corresponds with what is taken to be true.[7]

I do not think, however, that the ontological priority of the question of the meaning of Being over the sciences is the most significant reason why Heidegger thinks we should treat this question seriously. There is a far more important reason and that is the ontic priority of the questioner (though as we shall see in a moment this ontic priority is ontological). Let us remind ourselves about the structure of questioning for Heidegger. When I ask about something, I must, so to speak, begin somewhere. The question is which being do I start with? The detour through the sciences is really to underline that I cannot just start with any being, because such investigations only presuppose an ontology but cannot, on their own terms, address it. There is one being, however, who asks the question in the first place and that is myself. No doubt, I can be treated as though I were like any other being (this is what the sciences such as psychology and anthropology do, for example), but I am also very different from other beings, because I am the only being who is capable of asking what other beings are (the pencil does not ask what the light on my desk is). What Heidegger demonstrates is that such a gift, if that is what it is, is dependent upon the fact that my Being (not what I am, but the very fact that I am) can be an issue for me, which means that though I am a being, I am not just a being, and this is what Heidegger means when he writes, 'Dasein is ontically distinctive in that it *is* ontological' (BT: 32. Emphasis in the original).

Existence
If I am a being, what am I? First of all, before we can answer this question, let us reflect upon Heidegger's vocabulary, because he does not write 'human being', but 'Dasein'. Philosophers do not tend to invent new uses for words unless there is a very good reason to do so, and it is usually because they want us to look at our world in a different way. Words, like anything else, can become habits and thereby conceal more than they reveal. We all know what a human being is, and so to use the expression Dasein, which is usually left untranslated, is an attempt to break out of our preconceived ideas; and, as we already know from reading *Being and Time*, it is all about liberating us from a dead ontology preventing us from experiencing our world as it appears rather than as we think it should. In German, Dasein can just mean existence, and more specifically human existence, but dictionary definitions tell us nothing about the philosophical meaning of a word. Heidegger's use of the word 'Dasein' is much more specific than this. What it refers to is the ontological character of human existence, which is entirely lacking in any other being, and which is why this being may be the only way into the question of Being as such.

What can I mean by the expression 'ontological character'? Again, when we use philosophical terms, it can make everything appear esoteric and difficult, but what Heidegger is describing is an experience we all have, whether we are philosophers or not. My existence is a question for me. I worry about who I am, what I am doing, whether I am up to it at all. No doubt an animal can worry about where its next meal is coming from, but it does not worry about what it means to be an animal. My dog is not in anguish about what it is to be a dog; it just is. This is our tragedy, but it is also why we (unlike any other being) already have an understanding of Being, even if only in a confused way, because our Being is an issue for us and is always so. We are always caught up in the problem of our lives, even if we are running away from it. Science can give us no answers to these questions, because it can only tell me what I am, just as it can tell me what my dog is, but not how I am and why my existence as a whole matters to me. Even the scientist is a human being, and stands to his existence in the same way I do. Doing science is just one way of making sense of a life and giving it purpose, but 'making sense of a life' is not a scientific problem, but a human one.[8]

We tend to think of the word 'existence' applying to everything indiscriminately. We say the tree exists outside of my window, or the books on my table. But we also say ideas exist, like the idea of irrational numbers. We are even willing to entertain that fictional ideas exist (like unicorns), if only in our minds. For Heidegger, however, existence has a very precise and unique meaning in *Being and Time*. It applies only to the kind of being we are. Not in terms of our reality, if we mean by reality that we exist like everything else in the universe. Rather we exist because we have an understanding of our Being as the very basis of our Being. The question of Being does not have its roots in a philosophical doctrine for Heidegger. It rises up from our everyday experience of ourselves and our world. Being matters to me as a question because my own Being is important to me. Of course, it is the task of philosophy to make this implicit understanding of Being, which Heidegger describes as 'vague' and 'average', explicit. But this does not mean it leaves this experience behind to ascend the lofty heights of theory and contemplation. Our everyday experience of ourselves is always the guide of the meaning of our existence for Heidegger and it is this meaning which allows us to free ourselves from mistaken interpretations of Being.

When I say my life matters to me, I do not mean life in general, but my life. Existence, for Heidegger, as we remarked at the end of the Introduction, is supremely individual. Only I can live my life. Even if I decide to live like others, then it is still I who has decided to do so. These choices I make in my life, which are mine even if I disavow them, Heidegger describes through the neologism 'existentiell'. What is existentiell is an individual choice of someone, from as little as deciding to go to town in the afternoon, to becoming a physicist. The objective of the first two divisions of Part one of *Being and Time* is to describe the underlying existential structure of the existentiell.[9] Again philosophy takes the first investigation to be the most important, but without the existentiell, there would nothing to describe at all. The fact you are reading this book is an existentiell, that I wrote it in the first place, and even that philosophy exists is because one day someone decided to be a philosopher. Just as I can only understand Being through beings, then I can only understand the existential, the particular Being of Dasein, through the existentiell. As Heidegger writes, 'The roots of the existential analytic, on its part, are ultimately *existentiell* (BT: 34, Heidegger's emphasis).

The opposite to the existential understanding of Being is the categorical. The categorical understanding of Being relates to those beings which I encounter in the world. It is this kind of Being which is taught in philosophy classes through those strange kind of questions like, 'What is a chair?', 'How do I know the chair exists?' or even, 'How do I know what I say about the chair is true?'. All these are categorical questions. Heidegger does not dismiss them, rather he argues they are utterly inadequate to investigating the existential meaning of Being. I am not a chair. I do not exist in the same way a chair does, but a chair only exists because I do. Yet there are those who speak about me as though I really were the same as a chair. When someone reduces the meaning of my existence to the difference between my genes and that of an ape or a banana, then no matter how sophisticated and scientifically true their conversation with me is, they are still reducing my Being to the Being of a thing. They will say I am more complex than a chair, but none the less I am just a thing like every other thing in the universe. I am made of matter and atoms like everything else or if they want to be more poetic, we are all made from the same dust of the stars.

Such a discourse is not false when it restricts itself to the narrow scientific perspective, but it is wrong to assume there is only categorical Being or to confuse existential Being with it. I could live my life through the human genome project, base all my choices on it, and interpret the whole of my existence through it, but then it would no longer be a scientific theory about observable facts. It would be existential. Moreover, Heidegger would add, not only must we distinguish between the categorical and the existential, but the existential is more fundamental than the categorical. Chairs do not offer theories about the world. Science is a human activity. Like philosophy, it comes out of a particular way of Being in the world. Knowledge is a way we relate to things in attempting to comprehend them, but this relation is a particular way of existing in the world, and therefore the question of existence is more fundamental (ontologically speaking), than the problem of knowledge.

Two questions follow from this distinction between the existential and the categorical, and the priority of the former over the latter. First, why is it that I do interpret myself as a thing, and secondly, if I am not just a thing, what language can I use to describe who I am? In answer to the first question, as with the question of the meaning of Being itself, we must find the source for this error in our everyday experience of the world. Basically, as part of our very Being-in-the-world, we become so absorbed and involved with things that we come to interpret ourselves as though we were just like these things too. This everyday absorption, which Heidegger calls 'falling' (*Verfallen*), is further re-enforced by the philosophical tradition which offers us theories and hypotheses to support our self-misunderstanding, such that any other possible way of viewing our relation to ourselves and therefore to our world is almost impossible.[10]

One of Heidegger's most important tasks is to allow us to free ourselves from this tradition which is preventing us from experiencing our Being as it really is, rather than what we think it ought to be. He calls this task 'destruction', but as we shall see it is not as negative as it first might appear. It is not a matter of escaping our tradition completely, which Heidegger would think would be impossible anyway, but of seeing possibilities within it which it cannot see itself because of its own presuppositions and prejudices. What allows us, however, to see this bias invisible to it? Our guide is always the average everyday understanding of Being which we all possess. We do not counter theory with another theory, but with experience. Yet here we encounter another problem, possibly the most difficult of all. How can we account for or describe this experience when the only language in which we can talk about the world is categorical? If we are going to capture the existential as existential, then we cannot use the propositional language of predicates, attributes, concepts and categories. But it is precisely this language which we take to be the only true one.

How is Heidegger to surmount this problem? He will have to convince us there is a meaning of truth other than the categorical one. We have to wait until section thirty-three of *Being and Time* until we find out what this truth might be, but before we get there, and as a summary of where we have got to so far, we can already say there are three ways in which Heidegger tries to avoid describing the existential through the categorical, and they are all guided by the idea that it is our average everyday experience of the world which is the source for the meaning of Being. First of all, he uses ordinary language to describe our existence. Strangely enough, because we are so used to the technical language in philosophy, this sounds very obscure to our ears, and is one of the main reasons some have complained that Heidegger is too difficult. Secondly, as we saw from the introduction, he uses etymologies. Not so as to impress us with his knowledge of language, but to force us to rethink what our words mean in relation to our experience of ourselves and the world. Thus, if he reminds us of the etymology of the word 'Dasein', then it is not because, like some lexicographer, he is interested in words for their own sake, but this etymology (literally 'Dasein' means 'being there') makes us think again about what it means to be human, in the way that the definition 'rational animal' does not because we have become too comfortable with it. Finally, and this is perhaps one of the most contentious aspects of *Being and Time*, he uses religious language. Not because the rediscovery of ontology requires belief, but the description of religious experience might be closer to what it is to be human, than a metaphysics ossified through constant use.[11]

The Destruction of Philosophy

History is not something that lies outside of us, as merely a series of facts and events, but it affects the very sense of ourselves in the present. This explains why, even when I read, for example, an ancient text like Plato's *The Symposium*, it feels as though it were written yesterday. This is not because Plato and the ancient Greeks thought just like me and that all human beings do so. On the contrary, the way that I think about myself and the world has come down to me from them. For the most part, my relation to my tradition is unconscious, so much so that what were once the most difficult and abstract theories about existence have become common sense. Dislodging this common sense is the most difficult of all tasks, because it is hard for us to see there is even a problem. It has taken thousands of years of inculcation to make us think that the meaning of Being is not a serious question. So one of the first undertakings Heidegger has to perform is to show us that our common sense is not the result of our experience of the world, but is in fact the consequence of this tradition, which no longer affects us as a tradition at all but is just the way things are.

The source of our entrapment or bewitchment by the past belongs, as we have seen, in our relation to the world. In attempting to understand and control our external environment, we end up interpreting ourselves in the very same way as the things and objects we are involved with. In this way, the particular meaning of our existence is obscured and finally lost. It is this everyday relation to the world which is re-enforced by philosophy. It takes this everyday misinterpretation of existence and gives it a metaphysical stamp of approval. Take, for example, the metaphysics of Plato. His explanation of the Forms can be seen as an analogy to the activity of a craftsman. In order to make a shoe, I already need in my mind, in advance, the idea of a shoe to produce it. We begin with an everyday activity in the world (making things or production) and this ordinary relation to things becomes the representation of Being as a whole and the meaning of human existence. The whole universe, including myself, is the result of the creative activity of the *demiurge*.[12] This interpretation of Being as the Being of things is then subsequently repeated, with notable exceptions, throughout the whole of the history of philosophy, so that now it appears to us as just common sense.

How, then, can we dislodge this tradition? First of all we must take it seriously; which is why throughout Heidegger's career he constantly teaches and writes about the history of philosophy. This is not because he is interested in the history of philosophy for its own sake. He is not a scholar in this sense (and this is perhaps why sometimes other scholars get so angry with him). He does not read Descartes simply to understand him on his own terms, but rather how Cartesian metaphysics has come to be handed down in such a way that even it is no longer seen as problematic. This requires a twofold method which Heidegger calls 'destruction' (BT: 44).[13] This immediately sounds negative to our ears, as though we are supposed to turn our backs and forget about the past. This cannot be what Heidegger is suggesting, because the best way to ensure the past still has a hold upon us is by forgetting it. The first task of the destruction of the history of philosophy is to go back to the texts themselves and read them in detail to see how this metaphysical tradition has sustained and developed itself such that the question of the meaning of Being now appears totally irrelevant to us. From this first reading, however, necessarily follows the second, which is to show how these texts also always undermine and subvert themselves, and thereby indicate another way of thinking about the meaning of Being, one that will sustain the writing of *Being and Time* itself.

Heidegger gives an indication of this more positive side of the destruction of the history of philosophy through his allusion to Kant (BT: 45). What we discover, in reading the texts of philosophy, is that every ontology is an interpretation of time. This is no more so than in Kant's famous *Critique of Pure Reason*. It is time which acts as the bridge between understanding and sensibility, which are the two sides of human knowledge of the world.[14] None the less, for all Kant's proclamation in the preface and the introduction to his book that his thought marks a new beginning in the history of philosophy, for Heidegger, his ontology is merely a repetition of Descartes'. Kant's subject is still the subject of the *cogito*, and not Dasein. Even Descartes' ontology (despite his protestations) in the *Meditations* and the *Discourse on the Method* is a repetition of Scholastic thought, whose ontology has its basis in Aristotle.

The prejudice handed down over and over again through this tradition is that Being is always to be understood in terms of the present. As Heidegger writes, 'Entities are grasped in their Being as "presence"; this means that they are understood with regard to a definite mode of time – the "*Present*" (BT: 47. Heidegger's emphasis). Such an assumption places our involvement with things, and more specifically our theoretical grasp of things, over and above our existence, which must be the basis of this relation. The question is whether our existence can be understood through this priority given to the present. The whole aim of the second division of *Being and Time* is to show that the time of existence is not the same as the time of things. If the latter is the time of the present, then the former is the time of future, and if existence is to be the fundamental clue to the meaning of Being in general, then our ontology of time must also completely change.[15]

If we now go back to the structure of the question, we can fill in its three elements. What is being asked about (*Gefragtes*), is the meaning of Being. What is interrogated (*Befragtes*), is the existence of Dasein. And finally, what is discovered (*Erfragtes*), is time as the horizon of ontology. Heidegger's outline of *Being and Time* appears to follow the direction of this questioning (BT: 63–4). Originally, it was designed to be in two parts. The first part consisted of three divisions: the analytic of Dasein; the interpretation of time in relation to this analytic, and following from this interpretation, the meaning of Being in general in terms of time. The second part was meant to consist of the destruction of the history of philosophy from the perspective of the rediscovered temporal ontology, with one division each on Kant, Descartes and Aristotle. As anyone who has read *Being and Time*, and as many commentators have pointed out, only the first two divisions of part one were ever published. What we have in our hands, therefore, is only a fragment. Does this mean we can see it as a failure even before we have begun reading it? Perhaps, but let us remind ourselves that philosophy is about questions and problems more than answers and solutions, and the very fact that *Being and Time* is incomplete might be more absorbing than if it were. What is really interesting is the missing third division of the first part concerning time and Being. We can find the three divisions of part two published after *Being and Time* (either in lectures or published works), and perhaps Heidegger felt that it would be ridiculous to insert them back into the new editions, but not 'Time and Being'.[16]

Why is the last division of the first part missing? The Being of Dasein was meant to be the guide to the meaning of Being in general, but Heidegger never takes this step. Perhaps because his own interpretation of the relation between Dasein and the meaning of Being was too enmeshed in the tradition he was trying to escape. Does not

Heidegger's argument, in a curious way, repeat the traditional transcendental arguments which find the source of the world in the subject? And does not such a transcendental argument subvert (or at least is in tension with) the overall historical and concrete approach of *Being and Time*? How can Dasein be both historical and transcendental?[17]

Being-in-the-World

When we think of the world in which we live, we might imagine it to be a space we occupy in the very same way a thing is inside a bigger thing. Am I not in the world, to use Heidegger's example, as the water is inside the glass (BT: 79)? To think of our world in this way would be to confuse our way of Being with the Being of things, which is precisely what we should not do. I do not exist in the same way as the glass does. There is no doubt that I can be treated that way. In a certain way of looking at things, I too can appear as a thing. Seen in a photograph, I might seem to a casual observer to be merely in a room in the same way that water is in a glass. Even here, though, it is possible to look at the picture in a different way. The expression of my face might tell you how I felt at the time. Perhaps I look miserable or uncomfortable. Perhaps my world was not quite right with me. The expression 'my world', and the fact you understand it in a certain way, already tells you there is quite a difference between me and the water in the glass. In what sense can we say the water has its own world? Yet it is very easy for us to think about ourselves and others in this way. What else am I asking about when I meet you in the street and say, 'How are you?' Am I not asking about your world?

We have already seen from the previous part that Heidegger makes a fundamental distinction between categorical and existential Being. Human beings are not just things. One way they are not things is that their Being is an issue for them. A chair does not ask what it means to be a chair, but you can ask what it means to be you. But if I exist, what do I exist in? Chapters two and three of the first division of *Being and Time* are not only about interpreting this 'in' existentially and not categorically, but also demonstrating that the categorical meaning of Being rises out of the existential (or in Heidegger's language, the categorical is 'founded' upon the existential). It is only because things first matter to me (or the world is something that concerns me) that I want to know about them, and not the other way around. This is the complete reversal of the philosophical tradition which takes knowing to be primary and our concern for the world to be secondary and merely subjective and personal.

In this part we will be looking at the first three chapters of part one of the first division of *Being and Time*, whose overall argument can be divided into two key questions: 'What does it mean to exist?' and 'What does it mean to be in a world?' Heidegger also offers a detailed deconstruction of Descartes' account of nature (the only deconstruction in *Being and Time*, since Part two was never written) to show that it cannot make sense of how we live in the world, even though it is still the dominant scientific model of our age. Our own structure follows the articulation of Heidegger's argument and has been divided into three sections: 'Mineness', 'World' and 'Descartes and Spatiality'.

Mineness

The word 'existence' seems to be just as empty as the word 'Being'. Does it not merely refer to the banal fact that there is something? Thus, I say the chair exists, the table, the computer and so on. Everything exists in an undifferentiated way. Even I exist in the same manner that all other things exist. But this is not what Heidegger means by existence. For mere existence, he uses the Latin word *existentia* (BT: 67). But even this word has its origin in a dominant ontology of things that Heidegger wants to displace. Why should we think of the existence of things in this way? It is because a certain way of looking at things has been handed down to us from the past which we do not even think about any more, which is what it means to be is simply to be present in a uniform manner. Such a way of being, Heidegger calls 'present-to-hand' (*Vorhandensein*). But why should this be the only way in which things exist, and more importantly is this the way that I exist? Could there be a way of existing that is different, and specifically is Dasein such a different way of existing?

One way that Heidegger (in section nine [BT: 67–71]) distinguishes our way of existing from things is that I can talk about my existence as being mine. This goes back to what he already said in the introduction to *Being and Time* that the ontic priority (remembering that 'ontic' means that we are speaking about a specific being) of Dasein is that its Being is an issue for it (a dog does not worry about Being a dog; it just is one). Heidegger is not denying that my Being could not be of concern for others, but fundamentally if it were not so for me, then it would not be for others either. 'My being'(one possible translation for *Jemeinigkeit*, rather than mineness, as long as we understand Being here as a verb and not a noun – a way of Being and not a substantive) is the condition for the kind of care others have for me.[18]

How then are we to think about existence as something that could be mine? It is not a property we have, as when we say red is a property of a red thing. To think of existence as mine is to understand it in terms of possibilities. Stones do not have possibilities. The stone does not choose to be a stone. Animals do not have possibilities. My dog cannot wake up one day and decide not to be the dog it is. It acts through instinctual behaviour. I, however, can decide to be a student of philosophy, a doctor or a teacher or many other things. Of course my possibilities are not endless. I am a finite being, not an infinite one. An Aztec warrior could not have decided to become an astronaut, and if I am serious, I cannot really become an Aztec warrior (that is really be one). None the less, I still have to take a stand upon my existence, even if one way of doing so is to drift about in boredom and indecision.[19]

It is because Dasein's existence is understood in terms of possibilities and not properties, that every existence is singular. Everyone's existence is an issue for them individually. Of course, it is perfectly possible that we might face the same possibilities (and this is more than likely to be so since we share the same world), but how we face our possibilities and what they might mean to us is always going to be deeply personal. Later, in our reading of *Being and Time*, we will find that there is one possibility which we do all share, which is the possibility of our impossibility, which is our death.[20] What matters to Heidegger, however, is not the objective fact of our deaths (common to all life and not just human beings), but how each one of us, faces or does not face this possibility, since no one else can die our death. In other words, our Being towards this possibility is in every case our own.

But how can possibility be the distinguishing mark of Dasein's existence? Do I not also speak of things in the language of possibility? Think of the philosophers' famous example of the acorn and the oak tree. Do they not speak of the oak tree being the possibility of the acorn? Why is this any different from my possibilities? Precisely because we cannot talk of the acorn's possibility being its own. It is the same possibility for acorn A as it is for acorn B, and we cannot say that the one acorn lives its possibility differently from the other. It is true that in the course of time the development of one possibility might differ from the other. One acorn might have fallen on stony ground and never germinated, but this difference has to do only with external circumstances which belong indifferently to its existence and not with a relation of the acorn to its own possibility (and this is the case even if we think of something being wrong with the seed itself. It is not something it decides or chooses).

It is because the acorn exists indifferently towards its possibilities that it can be investigated scientifically. Human beings, as Heidegger points out in the following section, can also be objects of scientific study as in anthropology, psychology and biology, but then they are treated as though they were just complicated things, no different from any thing else which exists (BT: 71–5). It is precisely this way of looking at the world that Heidegger wants us to question. Why should we take this ontology to be the only true one? Moreover, the scientific viewpoint does not even take its own ontology seriously. It takes for granted that things exist and that we can speak about existence in the same way about everything, but it does not presume that this ontology is worthy of serious study.[21] What is lost in this ontology is the way of Being of human beings. I am like an acorn in that if do not eat or have water I will die, but I am not like an acorn, in that I can be a student, a teacher or even a reader of *Being and Time*. Even in relation to the first possibilities, if I think about it, I am not really like an acorn. For I have to ask myself why do I bother eating and drinking? What is it all for? What is the purpose and point of my life? This existential *telos* has nothing at all to do with nature (in fact nature has no purpose). It can only have a meaning in relation to an existence which can be called mine.

Of course, you might be thinking about the meaning of your life whilst you are reading this, but for the most part, if we are serious, we do not. In fact, for the most part we live like acorns (or perhaps like animals). We have no attitude to our possibilities at all. We just live them out of habit and ritual (I could tell you what I do every morning, and it does not change). Here Heidegger introduces one of the most important distinctions of *Being and Time*, between authenticity and inauthenticity (BT: 68). Again this is one of the places where knowing the German is useful. The word that is translated as 'authentic' is *eigentlich*, which derives from the adjective *eigen*, meaning 'own'. I can either own or disown my existence. I can choose to be who I am or just live my life without choosing at all. This is the real ontological difference between me and the acorn. It cannot choose to be its possibilities. It just is them, or they fail to happen. And this is the same for my dog. It just is its possibilities, or not. It might not wish to go for a walk in the pouring rain, but it cannot decide it does not want to live this life any more in its totality. I might suddenly despair being a student or a teacher, or any other human possibility, because I realise that I never made a decision to be this anyway, but just went ahead because everyone else did it.

Having made this distinction between authentic and inauthentic existence, we might think that Heidegger would use authentic existence as the template for what it is to be a human being, but he does not. On the contrary, he begins with average everyday existence (BT: 69). Authentic existence is something you or I choose in relation to our possibilities. I cannot begin with a specific possibility and then use it to define what it is to be a human being (let us say being a philosopher), for that would be to treat possibilities as properties which could be defined in advance, as when I define the perfect acorn as one that has a certain size, shape and colour in relation to which all other acorns are to be measured. Again, existence for Heidegger means 'ways of Being'. 'Ways of Being', so to speak, are personal (they are in each case something that we own or do not own). They are not a list of objective properties which we might find in a encyclopaedia or text book.

It is precisely this existence, the average and the everyday, which the philosophical tradition has passed over. Indeed, it has seen as its ultimate purpose and goal to get as far away from the everyday as possible. Plato would have said that the everyday belongs merely to 'opinion' (*doxa*). Today we might think of it as 'subjective', which has nothing at all to do with the truth of things. What we want to know is the objective world of facts and principles, and not the everyday worries and anxieties of people (and even if we are interested in these, then we want to know about them objectively). This is to think of our existence as a derivative of the Being of things, and not, as Heidegger wants to show us in the two chapters that follow, the Being of things as descended from ours. Things only have a meaning because we already exist in a world, and this world belongs to our everyday existence, even though philosophy, and the science that comes from it, continually confuses the world with a thing when they interpret it as nature.

World
As we have already remarked, we can speak about Being in two ways for Heidegger, either categorically and existentially.[22] The first belongs to things and the second to the Being of Dasein. Western philosophy (since Aristotle) has continually confused the latter with the former. One way of thinking of the difference between these two ways of Being is through the simple proposition 'in'. When we say we exist in a world what do we mean by the word 'in'? Is not inhabiting a world like one thing being inside another thing, but on a bigger scale? We remember the childhood cartoon of a boy who is sitting on a boat in a lake, and then the view keeps moving further back from the town, to the country, to the world, and finally to the universe, as though existing were the same as being inside one thing after the other until we come to the largest thing which is the universe (we even wonder what might be outside of the universe). However moving and wondrous this picture might be, it is entirely inappropriate to the Being of Dasein. It confuses our way of Being with the Being of things. It is the water in the glass which exists in this Russian doll universe, not us. Of course, viewed from a scientific way of looking at things, we can be seen in this way, but it is Heidegger's argument that this is not fundamental to our way of Being. We exist as a 'who' and not as a 'what' (BT: 71).

It is very hard to stop thinking about ourselves as things, but Heidegger uses another example of a chair to help us (BT: 81). Our relation to our world is not like the relation to a thing in space. The world is something in which we exist, but 'in' here does not mean being inside something, but 'being alongside'.[23] Heidegger interprets 'being alongside' in the more primary sense of familiarity. I am in the world as being at home. The world is where I live, and living in the world is quite different from water being in a glass. One way in which my world is familiar to me is that I encounter things within it which are part of my everyday experience. The cup, the kettle and the teapot, for example, which are part of my morning ritual; without which, I commonly say to others, I would not be able to function. I encounter these things in my world, but one thing we can say about things is that they do not encounter other things. We can say the chair is touching the wall which it is leaning against, but there really is not an encounter between them, but only a spatial relation of contiguity.

How then do we relate to the world, if we do not do so as a thing is next to another thing? Again we have to go back to our everyday experience to provide the clue. This is to reverse the whole trajectory of the history of philosophy, which tends to understand the question of the existence of the world as one of knowledge. It imagines that I am a worldless being which somehow has to get outside of itself in order to find the world. For Heidegger, on the contrary, I am already in the world, and the problem of the existence of the external world begins only if you understand the Being of Dasein as the same as the Being of things. This is the primary way, as we saw in the introduction, that Heidegger differs from his teacher Husserl. For the latter takes epistemology, which is the problem of knowledge of the external world, as being the basic question of philosophy. Heidegger would say to Husserl that Dasein first of all has to exist before it can know anything. In the language of section thirteen of *Being and Time* (which ironically in this case is taken from Husserl), knowing is a 'founded' mode of existence (BT: 86).

In this way of thinking about the world (which has its origin in Descartes), the relation between the world and Dasein is thought through the difference between a subject and an object. In epistemology, the world is understood as external nature which in some strange and peculiar sense is 'out there'. The single most important problem of epistemology is how do we get from the inner sphere of the subject to the outer sphere of nature, since both are entirely different kinds of being. Although epistemology does think of the subject and the object as being different, it leaves this difference totally obscure. *Being and Time* throws light on this darkness by asking the question directly, 'What does it mean to be the kind of being that I am?'

As long as I am not seduced by metaphysics, I can see I exist along-side the world as something which is familiar to me. The world is not an alien object where I somehow have to wonder about how I got there and how I relate to it. I am my world as that which is intimate to me, to the extent that the world, in my everyday existence, is not a problem for me at all. This relation to the world can only be understood, Heidegger argues, through an ontology of care, which is more primordial than the abstract knowledge of things. Things first of all matter to me in a world I care about.[24] Only in a second moment, do I have a relation to them in terms of knowing. Knowledge, rather than being the essential relation to things, as metaphysics interprets it, is secondary. To know something is to hold ourselves back from our normal involvement in the world. This is why philosophical examples sound so peculiar and alien, as when a teacher addresses a student and points to a chair and says 'What is it?' We do not really relate to chairs in this way when we go about our world, and it is only because the philosopher speaks about things in this odd way that the world suddenly becomes a problem for us.

In the example of perception as our model of the relation to the world, the context of my experience is stripped away. We are left with the empty existential correlation of the eye with a thing (where the eye itself is just seen as another thing): this chair, this table, this room and so on until again we end up with the universe. But my primary relation to things is that they matter to me. The table is for putting something on, the chair for sitting and the room for listening to lectures. The epistemological problem of the world is a false one. It is not that Heidegger (in section thirteen) proves that the world exists in a better way than Descartes, Kant or Husserl, rather he shows that the question is nonsensical as soon as we realise that the Being of Dasein is not the same as the Being of a thing (BT: 86–90). We do not have to get from an 'inside' to an 'outside' to understand our relation to the world, because we are already outside of ourselves in our involvement with things which matter to us.

We need to think in a deeper way, then, exactly what we mean by the expression 'world' and this is how Heidegger begins chapter three, 'The Worldhood of the World'. I know that I relate to things outside of me (houses, trees, people, mountains, stars, Heidegger writes), but is the world just a collection of these things (BT: 91)? By simply making a list of things, the meaning of the world is in fact concealed from us because we end up thinking of it as a thing. We conceive of the world as a container in which things like houses, trees, people, mountains and stars simply exist, and we end up calling this container 'nature' or 'the universe'. Rather than understanding the world through the nature, we need to understand nature through the world, but we can only do so if we equally understand the world existentially and not categorically. This would mean that rather than the world being a category of things (the physical space in which they are found) it is an existential way of Being of Dasein. It is because Dasein has a world, or having a world belongs essentially to its way of Being, that things like houses, trees, mountains and stars also have a world (one way of which is Being in nature).

Heidegger tells us in section fourteen that there are four ways of speaking about the world (BT: 93):

1. As an ontical concept which expresses the totality of beings. What is meant by the words 'nature' or 'cosmos'.
2. Ontologically, as the way of Being of these beings which are defined above.
3. Ontically again, but as the world of a particular Dasein.
4. Finally ontologically, as what it means for any Dasein to belong to a world. What Heidegger calls 'worldhood' (*Weltlichkeit*).

The meaning of the world that concerns Heidegger in *Being and Time* is the last one: the ontological significance of the world which belongs to Dasein. A world, (the world that you or I live in) is cultural and historical, specific to a people and can live and die. What we are interested in, however, is the general meaning of the world, which is true of every world, whether we are thinking about our world today or the world of the Aztecs in the sixteenth century. But how are we to get to this world which is at the bottom of every world? The answer to this question again is our everyday experience, for only in this way can we break through the assumptions which prevent us from understanding the world correctly. The world that is closest to us Heidegger calls the 'environment', which in German is *Umwelt*, the world which surrounds us.

To 'see' this everyday world, we must describe how things we encounter really present themselves in our dealings with them, and fight against our temptation to over-interpret them, for example, in the models of perception. We must follow, in other words, what Heidegger has already described as the phenomenological method: interpret what you see as it shows itself in itself.[25] We relate to things first of all because they matter to us and not because we need to know what they are in the abstract way in which philosophy describes them. For this reason, we first of all encounter things, Heidegger tells us in section fifteen, not as objects of knowledge but as 'tools' or 'equipment' (*Zeug*) which are useful for us (BT: 97). Moreover, we never just encounter one piece of equipment in isolation, like the chair or table which the philosopher points to in her lectures. Rather, one item of equipment always refers to another one. I open the door in order to leave the room. I walk down the corridor in order to leave the building. I leave the building in order to buy a cup of coffee and so on. Thus, unlike in perception, I do not see a thing as separate from everything else, rather things are tools which always relate to other things. This experience of the interrelation between equipment (what Heidegger calls their 'assignment' or 'reference') should not be confused with a mere collection of things (as when we thought of the world as container in which things like houses, trees, people, mountains and stars simply exist). Rather, I am at home with them. I do not enter a room and start counting things and measuring the distance between them. I do not experience the room first of all as a geometrical but as a living space where things relate to each other in terms of my everyday dealings with them.

I go into my living room. I switch on the television with my remote control and sit down on my sofa and watch (absent-mindedly, perhaps) the programme. All these things are present to you now reading this (you might even be imagining your own living room), but when you think of it in the actual action itself are these things ever present? They are present now in my recollection of it, but ordinarily I do not notice the television or the remote control or the sofa. Things disappear in their use. I do not have a theory of my living room. I just make use of it. It is not looking at the hammer, Heidegger tells us, which reveals the being of the hammer as a tool, but hammering (BT: 98).

We must sharply distinguish, therefore, between what is present as an object of knowledge (what Heidegger calls *Vorhandensein* – present-to-hand) from what reveals itself or does not reveal itself in use

(*Zuhandensein* – ready-to-hand). No matter how hard I look at the hammer, I can never disclose its 'ready-to-handness'. As soon as something is called to my attention, then it becomes present-to-hand. The hammer ceases to be a 'hammering nails into the wood in order to build a house', but is simply a hammer with certain properties. What concerns me when I use something is not the thing itself, but the purpose which it fulfils. I am watching television because I am tired or even to avoid the work I am supposed to be doing.

The whole drive of Heidegger's analysis in sections fifteen and sixteen is to show that my everyday involvement with things already involves and implies a world. My relation to things takes place in my activity which only makes sense through my existence and which in turn only has a meaning within a world. All of this he calls the 'towards which' of equipment which makes up its network of references or assignments (BT: 99). The reason why the phenomenon of the world is so difficult to see, and why we can understand that it is so easy to confuse it with nature, is that it is invisible in two ways: firstly, in the scientific and philosophical model of perception where things are ripped out of their context and simply looked at; and secondly, in my everyday involvement with things where, because I am so occupied, the world disappears into the background. As I slump in front of my television, it is highly unlikely that I will notice my world.[26] It only becomes visible when it is interrupted.[27]

We can imagine Heidegger's phenomenology as a making explicit of what occurs in these breaks. Every night I walk into my room and switch on the television at a certain time. One day I do the same and the television does not work. Suddenly, in that moment, the meaning of my world reveals itself. What is made visible is the interrelation between things. My world is not one of them, but the relation between them – the significance of my world. This significance, which is more like a flavour than a concept, is neither present, nor ready-to-hand. On the contrary, it refers back to my existence.

The world as the interrelationship of things is further reinforced in section seventeen through the analysis of signs (BT: 107–83). Signs are important for Heidegger not because they are not just symbols or indicate something, but because they reveal the world in which we live. In one sense, all equipment is a sign, because every piece of equipment refers to another piece of equipment whose interlocking is given a significance through a world which for the most part is invisible to those who participate in it, because it is simply part of 'getting around'. Heidegger's example is the indicator of car (which at the time he was writing would have been a small red arrow) (BT: 108–9). The position of the red arrow determines the direction in which the car will move at a crossroads and is controlled by the driver. In this way, the indicator is a tool which has a use within the general context of driving, not only for the driver but for other drivers as well. We might say the red arrow indicates I am turning left or right. This indication, however, Heidegger asserts, is not primary. To make sense of this indication I have to refer to a deeper ontological structure which he calls 'serviceability' (*Dienlichkeit*) (BT: 109).

Signs indicate because they first of all provide a service. They do not provide a service because they indicate. What then is the source of the service signs provide? It is ourselves. If we did not need to indicate turning to the left or the right (or we did not live in a world in which such an action made sense), then there would be no indicators. Or look at it this way: there would be no indicators on cars if there were not intersections; there would be no intersections if there were not roads; but there would be no roads if human beings did not make journeys. And why do we make journeys? Here we are beginning to ask the important ontological question about the world. We make journeys because we have projects. I might be running away from something, or I could just be going to work or delivering the post. We might even imagine an existential journey, a great line of flight which is so common to much American literature and film. In each case, whether consciously or not, every journey expresses the way in which someone takes a stand or interprets his existence. It is a way to be.

Signs reveal the world in which I live which is the basis of equipmentality. This world is not nature, if we imagine by this word the mathematical representation of geometrical space. The first part of section eighteen acts as a summary of all that we have so far hopefully understood (BT: 114–22). My everyday involvement with things already involves a world, even though this might not be explicit to me. This world is not a thing (it is neither present or ready-to-hand) but is the context in which my use of things makes sense, what Heidegger calls its 'towards which' and 'for which' (BT: 114). Such purposes are not properties of things, rather they refer back to the being of Dasein, whose possibilities link things together. To use Heidegger's example, I would not be hammering this nail into this piece of wood, if I were not making this hut in order to secure myself against the vagaries of the weather (BT: 116). The fundamental 'towards which', therefore, is the 'in order to' of Dasein.

Any particular involvement with a thing only makes sense within a totality of involvements. The question 'Why am I building this hut?' can only be answered through what my world means to me, but this world is not something that stands outside of me like a thing. Indeed, it is not a 'something' at all. Rather it is the basic familiarity that I have with things. Such an involvement is not a theoretical reasoning, in which things appear in front of me like snapshots, but the way in which I am comfortable with my surroundings. Being-in-the-world, therefore, is not a property which Dasein could choose or not choose to have. It belongs ontologically to what Dasein is. Without this world which every Dasein, so to speak, carries along with itself in its involvement with things, things themselves would neither be present nor ready-to-hand. My world illuminates or gives significance to things (in Heidegger's language, it 'frees' them to be what they are).

The metaphysical tradition, and the scientific world view that is sustained by it, even if unconsciously, takes the world, on the contrary, to be a physical thing of which Dasein is just one thing amongst others. We have to understand this perspective, and more importantly its ontological deficiencies, because it blocks our own understanding of what the world really is. Heidegger's example of such a mistaken view is Descartes.

Descartes and Spatiality

We remember that for Heidegger it is not possible to get back to our experience of the world without 'destroying' the tradition which clouds our own understanding. The history of philosophy is not just the dusty shelves of books in a library, but affects the way all of us think. This is why the second part in the plan of *Being and Time* was meant to be a destruction or deconstruction of three of the most important thinkers of this tradition: Kant, Descartes and Aristotle. We know that Heidegger never completed this part, but most of it was achieved in other publications. None the less in this section of *Being and Time* ('A contrast between our analysis of worldhood and

Descartes' Interpretation' [BT: 122–34]), Heidegger gives a clear indication of what his treatment of Descartes would have been if he had written the second part.

We might also ask ourselves the question, why Descartes and not some other philosopher? The answer to this question is twofold: first, Descartes is important because he is the mainstay or foundation of our scientific conception of the world as nature; and second, (perhaps more importantly), his has become the common sense interpretation of the world, even amongst those who have not read a word of philosophy or have even heard the name Descartes. Such a view of the world is just taken to be true, even though it runs counter to our own experience of ourselves. The aim of Heidegger's destruction is to show how Descartes' description of nature is ontologically inadequate in understanding our world, but also to show the superiority of own existential analysis in this task. It ends, therefore, with the existential explanation of space, which we can contrast with the geometrical one.

What is at fault in the Cartesian interpretation of the world is a confusion of ontological difference. It translates an ontic definition of things into an ontological explanation of the world. In other words, it takes a scientific description of things to be equivalent to our experience of the world, but as we have seen the world is not a thing, whether ready or present-to-hand, but the way of Being of Dasein. How then does Descartes understand the nature of things? He comprehends them through the metaphysical concept of extension, which is essentially spatial. The fundamental distinction, Heidegger asserts, in Descartes' philosophy is between nature and spirit (BT: 123). The difference between them is internal to the idea of substance. Nature is material and spirit immaterial. The essential attribute of nature is extension, which is the real being of the world. All that exists is a mode of extension, including shape and motion and all other properties of matter. What is at the heart of this metaphysical conception of the world is the notion of Being as permanence, but as Heidegger has already pointed out to us, this is not something new at all but has its source in Parmenides' interpretation of Being as 'that simple awareness of something present-to-hand in its sheer present-to-hand' (BT: 48). Ontologically speaking, Descartes is not revolutionary at all, even though he presents himself as so being, but is merely the continuation of a long metaphysical tradition which began with the ancient Greeks.

It is we who are reading Descartes, after going through the analytic of Dasein, who are aware of his ontological presuppositions. He, on his part, is completely ignorant of them, and like those to whom the opening pages of *Being and Time* are addressed, no longer takes Being as a serious philosophical question, because it is defined as substance which is said to be inaccessible. It is marked by a theological silence. The world is interpreted as extension, but the ontology of substance is left unclear. This substance itself is interpreted ontically, such that the difference between the ontological and the ontic is also left unclear, but it is precisely this difference which is the key question and problem.

What we have to understand is that Descartes' ontology is not an ontology of the world at all, since extension can only be thought through a thing. The world is just one type of thing amongst other things. We have to ask ourselves how Descartes has ended up with such a distorted picture of the world. It is because he takes the scientific understanding of things as the only possible relation to the world. What is at the heart of this mathematical physics is the ontology of the present-to-hand, where the world, as the way of being of Dasein, is completely invisible. What matters to him is only how we know things, and not Being. His assumptions predetermine his description of the appearance of phenomenon, rather than letting them appear as they show themselves. Everything is reduced to a mathematical figure. This is not to deny the truth of mathematics, but it is to accuse Descartes of confusing a regional with a general ontology. The language of mathematics tells us something about mathematical objects but not about the meaning of Being in general.

Not only does Descartes' explanation leave us completely in the dark about what the world is, it also obscures the Being of Dasein. For it too is interpreted through the metaphysical category of substance. True, it is conceived through thought and not extension, but such a way of thinking about Dasein makes it absolutely impossible to understand our practical involvement with things in the world which is the everyday basis of our existence. The philosopher comes up with a picture of the world which has nothing at all to do with how we live, and then we are supposed to drop our profound sense of ourselves for their narrow truth. Descartes compresses the meaning of the world to the ontology of things which are present-to-hand whose only access is through mathematical formulas; but what does this have to do with how we really experience the world? Am I computing mathematical equations when I reach out for a glass in order to drink some water? Am I calculating a series of zeros and ones, when I say to someone that I love them? When we think about it, what a peculiar view of human beings this is, even though we take mathematics, and the science which is based upon it, to be the only true interpretation of the world.[28]

That Descartes passes over the phenomenon of the world is not an error on his part, but belongs essentially to the way that Dasein relates to the world. We become so involved with things that we begin to interpret ourselves as though we were just like them. It is also a way of fleeing from our Being and our responsibility for ourselves. Such an experience of our Being also becomes justified by the philosophical tradition, which takes this inauthentic way of being and sets it into stone as the true picture of the world. Any ontical science (however interesting and true it might be on its own terms) cannot be an answer to an ontological question. We have seen that the world is grounded in the way Dasein exists, and not in some mysterious properties of things which are taken as a fact. For even science, and the way that it investigates things, must first of all come from the way Dasein exists. After all, scientists themselves are human beings.

How then does Dasein exist in space, if it does not do so as a thing? This question is answered by the last part of chapter three, 'The Aroundness of the Environment, and Dasein's Spatiality' (BT: 134–48). Hopefully, we already recognise now that if we are going to understand Dasein's spatiality, then we have to do so through our practical involvement with things and not through a supposedly 'objective' knowledge of them. It is phenomenologically incorrect to suggest that things which are ready-to-hand are related to us through the abstract space of geometry. Things are near and far to the extent we are involved and interested in them and not because of the mathematical distance between us. Existentially speaking, the laptop into which I am typing these words is closer to me than the glasses that are on the end of my nose which I never notice, even though in terms of measured distance the glasses are closer to me than the laptop

(Heidegger's example is spectacles and a picture of the wall [BT: 141]).

Such practical places are not an objective property of things or of the world understood as nature, but belong to the existence of Dasein. It is I who give places to things, not things that place me, and things only have their places or 'regions', as Heidegger calls it, because they matter to me (BT: 136). Something is near or faraway from me, not because of an objectively measured distance, but because of my concern for it. Moreover, the objective distance between things would only be significant for me if I was already involved in them. The objective distance between the Earth and the Sun is only significant and intelligible because understanding the solar system is something of great interest to us. This is not to reduce the objective distance between things to a mere subjective phenomenon. There really is 150,000,000 kilometres between the Earth and the Sun, but such a fact is ontical and not ontological. What we have to ask ourselves is why such a fact interests us and if this is the only way to relate to the Sun.[29]

Dasein's primary interest in things Heidegger calls 'de-severance' and 'directionality' (BT: 138). De-severance is the English translation of the German word *Ent-fernung*. Heidegger uses the hyphen to emphasise the idea that in taking interest in things Dasein removes the distance between it and them. It does so because of its own projects and possibilities. Equally, things have a direction only in relation to me, whether we take direction in a limited sense as being left and right or in the more fundamental sense of the 'in order to'. It belongs to Dasein's way of being that it brings, both practically and theoretically, things close to itself. In one sense, this expresses the familiarity and intimacy of our world, where everything has its place, but as modern technology, it can also lead to the destruction of the mystery of things, where paradoxically the removal of distance only has the consequence of defamiliarisation:

In Dasein there lies an essential tendency towards closeness. All the ways in which we speed things up, as we are more or less compelled to do today, push us on towards the conquest of remoteness. With the 'radio', for example, Dasein has so expanded its everyday environment that it has accomplished a de-severance of the 'world' – a de-severance which, in its meaning for Dasein, cannot yet be visualised. (BT: 140. Heidegger's emphasis)[30]

In summary, the world is always there in some way for us. We are not 'worldless' beings, as philosophy sees us, which somehow have to find our way back into a world. We already live in a world. We are already outside of ourselves in a world. This world is not the world of knowledge and cognition, but of practical involvement and concern. Indeed, it is this world which is the condition for knowledge. If our world were not something which mattered to us, then we would not investigate and inquire into things. But the world is not a thing, and we are not things which are inside a larger thing. The world is the way of Being of Dasein. Its only meaning is Dasein's understanding of itself. It is a web of meaning through which we discover our orientation and direction. Such a web, as Dreyfus constantly reminds us, cannot be an object of knowledge, because it is not something we have to know or believe in.[31] On the contrary, to have a belief or to know something requires that this web already exists. The world is the background significance of all our everyday practices from which everything that is of concern and interest to us springs, including philosophy.

Others, Language and Truth

Heidegger already speaks of others when he describes the Being of equipment and the relation to the world which is visible there. So as not to clutter up my own analysis with too much material, I did not directly refer to them. How then are others already there when I am working with or using things? They are present in the fundamental 'in order to' of Dasein's Being. In relating to things as ready-to-hand, I already related to those others which Heidegger says belong to the 'public world' (BT: 100). Just as much as the problem of the existence of the world is a headache which has been induced by too much philosophy, so too is the existence of other minds.[32] The origin of this view has its source in the same metaphysics which sees the world as having a thing like nature. As we have seen, we cannot understand Dasein's Being through such a conception as though it were merely a thing. Just as much as I am not in the world like water in a glass, then others are not separate from me. My relation to others already belongs to the way that I am, and I cannot understand my own Being apart from them. I am with them from the very beginning.

If in this chapter we shall look more specifically at how Heidegger describes our relation to others in our everyday world, we shall also examine his deepening of analysis of how Dasein is in the world. The difference between chapter five, 'Being-In as Such', and chapter three, 'The Worldhood of the World', is that 'being-in' is now described primarily through moods, language and understanding and not our practical relation to things in the world. If Dasein's Being is characterised as 'Being-in the-world', then so far we have only investigated the world. Our next task, therefore, is to analyse the 'Being-in' of Dasein, how and in what way we live in a world. In the previous chapter, this was for the most part described negatively. Dasein does not live in the world in the way that a thing occupies space. Now, our question is positive: what is the determinate way in which Dasein is in a world? Increasingly, the object of fundamental ontology becomes the particular way of Being of Dasein (what makes us different from any other beings), until it culminates in the famous description of 'Being-towards-death' in the opening pages of the second division.

This part is divided into three sections: 'The They', 'Moods, Understanding and Language' and finally 'Truth'. Hitherto our order of explanation (apart from our jumping ahead to phenomenology in the introduction) has followed the order of *Being and Time*. Now, since it fits better with the topics themselves, we are going to leap forward to the interpretation of truth in section forty-four. This is without doubt one of the most important sections in *Being and Time*. Heidegger returns again and again to this theme in his later writings, and it is the key to comprehending his notion of Being.[33] I shall leave my discussion of 'falling' until the beginning of the next part.

The They

Just as with the distinction between the authentic and the inauthentic, we should not take the difference between myself and others as being a moral or social one. Heidegger is not bemoaning the fact that none of us today is really an individual (of course, as everyone knows, those who shout loudest that they are individuals are always the ones who are least so), but is describing the way of Being of Dasein. It belongs essentially to Dasein's Being that it is already with others in the world. It is for this reason that we have already come across the phenomenon of others in the description of the world as our environment in which we pursue our daily tasks. It does not matter whether I am with others or not in the factual sense, for whatever I do already indicates the presence of others, even if they are absent. In writing this book now, I am already in relation to the others who will read it, though of course it would be profoundly uncomfortable if these others were actually in my room as I write. If Heidegger does make a social comment, so for example when he remarks that in our everyday existence we tend to 'read, see and judge about literature and art as *they* see and judge' (BT: 164. Heidegger's emphasis), he does not mean by this that it is a modern curse which we have somehow to throw off, but that understanding ourselves in this way is part of our everyday existence. The ontological analysis must come first, otherwise *Being and Time* would just be sociological treatise in a very limited sense, as merely an interesting list of opinions about the modern world which we might suspect are only the opinions of the researcher. No doubt from the ontological analysis we might make social comments (and Heidegger certainly does), but such statements do not invalidate the ontology.

What then is at issue in Heidegger's analysis of the 'They' (or the 'Anyone' as some others translate the German, *Das Man*)? It is the answer to the question, who is Dasein. Now we might have thought we had already answered this question, when Heidegger wrote at the beginning of division one that Dasein is in each case 'mine' (BT: 68). We remember that what distinguishes existence from the mere existing of a thing is that my existence is something I have to accomplish. Rather than just being given, it is a drama or task. So why do we have to talk about the They? Precisely because existence is a drama and not just a definition of something. I have to struggle to make my existence mine. It is a possibility I can have or lose. It is not an actuality which belongs to a thing as part of its definition (as a triangle has three sides). If I have to make my existence mine, then there must be something against which I have to fight, and this is the meaning of the They.

Again we have to be very careful not to read this as a moral lack on my part, as though Heidegger were making a statement that it is terrible that so many people do not live individual lives any more (which must be one of the most inauthentic statements ever uttered). Dasein's involvement and absorption in the world, as we have already seen, is not a failure on its part, but is the very way in which we exist in the world. Such everyday existence is anonymous, and it is from this background that I have to wrest my own singularity (a singularity, which we shall see when we come to look at anxiety, has nothing at all to do with individuality, if we mean by the latter being different or unusual). Or, to put it in Heidegger's more technical vocabulary, Dasein's self is a modification of the 'They-self' and not the other way around (BT: 168).

So strangely enough the answer to the question, 'Who am I?' is not first of all an 'I' or a 'self' , because I do not live as an isolated subject which somehow has to find its way back into the world. There is no fundamental ontological opposition between self and others. On the contrary, others already belong to very Being of Dasein. Being with others is not a secondary characteristic added onto my existence. I am already with others from the very beginning. The traditional philosophical problem of other minds is absurd because it presupposes that Dasein is a closed entity like a thing which is present-to-hand. Existentially speaking, the existence of others is not a problem at all, because by the very fact that I am in the world I am already involved with others. I do not have to prove they exist to make sense of them, because I cannot make sense of myself without them.

My original ontological relation to others Heidegger names as 'Being-with' (*Mitsein*). Being-with is just as significant as Being-in in understanding the Being of Dasein. Just as we must understand the 'in' of Being-in specifically in an existential way, then we should also understand the 'with' of Being-with. 'With' here does not have a categorical meaning, as one thing being next to another thing. The 'I' and the 'Other' are not two things opposed to one another. Quite the contrary, I am with others precisely because we do not stand apart from one another. I am with others because we share the same concern with the world. Things cannot share a world in this way, just as the chair, in Heidegger's previous analysis, cannot encounter the wall it is leaning against (BT: 81). I do not relate to others, therefore, as a theoretical or social construct examined from the outside by an anthropologist or sociologist. Rather in my everyday involvement in the world, they are already there with me. As Heidegger writes in section twenty-six, even when I walk alongside a field in the countryside, and nobody is there, others are still present as Being-with, because the boundaries of this field mattered to someone at sometime, and my walk itself traces the contours of their concern (BT: 153). Thus, it is ridiculous to claim Dasein does not already belong to others in its very existing, because it can be alone. I can only be alone because I am already with others. Why would loneliness affect me so if this were not the case?

If I do encounter others already in my environment, this does not mean others have the same Being as things. Others, as those which already belong to my Being, are neither present nor ready-to-hand, rather they are like me. This is why, in section twenty-six, Heidegger will use the word 'solicitude' (*Fürsorge*) rather than 'concern' to describe the specific nature of my relation to others (BT: 157). In my everyday existence, I am indifferent to the presence of others. I walk down the street and I hardly see them at all, just as I do not see the door I walk through every day unless it is locked against my expectations. Such an indifferent relation to others, however, is still a relation, even if it is a privative one. I can only ignore others in this way because they are part of my everyday existence.

Heidegger also writes, however, that I can have a positive relation to others, where they are present to me, though not in the way that a thing is, and this positive relation has two forms: one, where I stand in or replace the other's possibilities; and two, where I free others for their own possibilities. It will not be entirely clear to us until the next section what Heidegger means by 'possibility' here, but it is perfectly clear what he means by standing in or freeing the other. If my purpose in writing this book is to release you from the effort of reading Heidegger's *Being and Time*, then it could be said I am standing in for you. If, on the contrary, my original intention was to enable you to understand *Being and Time* better for yourself, then it might be argued I am freeing you to be yourself, rather than substituting your own understanding for mine. Solicitude also has its own way of seeing parallel to the circumspection of concern where 'one looks after others', which Heidegger calls 'considerateness' and 'forbearance' (BT: 159). Again such a 'seeing' should not be confused with theoretical knowledge. I do not first of all know others, rather they matter to me, and only in this way would knowing something about them be significant at all.

Others also, and this is more predominantly the case, rule over the possibilities of Dasein, but not as some particular of specific 'Other', as in the case of solicitude. It is these others, which are always hazy and indistinct and really no one at all, which Heidegger calls the 'They' or the 'Anyone'. I see myself as others see themselves ('We take pleasure,' as Heidegger writes, 'and enjoy ourselves as *they* take pleasure; we read, see and judge about literature and art as *they* see and judge' [BT: 164. Heidegger's emphasis]). What is important, however, about these others is they are not anyone specific; they are just someone. I could not really point to them in the street and say it is they who are determining the way I engage with the world. On the contrary, these opinions and ways of living are just in the air with no one being responsible for them at all. This anonymity is inseparable from a 'levelling down' of possibilities, because we cannot really find the source for why everyone thinks or acts in this way so no one has to be accountable for their existence.[34]

In Dasein's absorption and involvement in the world, in its comparison of itself with those who share its world, it takes on the characteristic of the They. Rather than being itself it is this anonymous self. The who of Dasein's existence, therefore, is not a self, first of all, but a 'they-self'. I think, act and do what everyone else thinks, acts and does. Again we have to be very careful not to mistake this analysis for a moral crusade on Heidegger's behalf. It is part of the very way Dasein exists that it is absorbed in the world, and also shares this world with others. The fact that I myself, for the most part, live my life as others do, without regard or introspection, belongs essentially to my Being. It is not a personal fault. It does mean, however, if I am to be myself and not a 'they-self' (it is important to underline that being a 'they-self' is a way to be me, and does not contradict the existential fact that existence is always 'mine'), then this will always be against the background of anonymous existence. The self is not given to Dasein. It is something it has to win. As I wrote at the beginning of this section, life is a drama and a struggle. It is a task to be accomplished and not merely a fait accompli. How such a possibility is possible, we can only see by the deepening of the analysis of Being-in-the-world through the description of moods and the understanding.

Moods, Understanding and Language
So far I have described Being-in-the-world through our involvement with equipment and our intimacy (indifferent for the most part) with

others. Both these ways of Being, however, are dependent on a more fundamental structure of existence. We remember from the previous chapter that the 'being-in' of Dasein is not the same as the 'being-in' of beings which are present-to-hand. The spatiality of Dasein is not geometrical, but lived. As when, for example, we speak of someone being close to us. We do not mean by this the smallness of the distance between us (except metaphorically), but that they are important to us.[35] Thus, someone on the other side of the world (existentially speaking) can be closer than the person sitting right next to us on the bus. The way in which equipment and others are related to me is therefore dependent on my own 'position' in the world. This position is, again, not a geometrical one, but belongs to my own way of existing in the world. Heidegger calls it (evoking the literal German meaning of the *da* of Dasein) the 'there', which is to be grasped as 'disclosure' (*Erschlossenheit*) (BT: 171).

When I relate to equipment and others, I reveal their Being (this is what Heidegger means when he occasionally says that Dasein frees beings). In so doing, I bring them into my world. Such a world is not a place on a map (at least not directly), but a horizon of intelligibility in which equipment and others make sense and have a presence for me. We can imagine (as long as we do not take this literally), the 'there' of Dasein as an illuminated circle in which equipment and others are lighted up. Of course this luminescence is not solitary, but one which I share with others. None the less I have to, so to speak, live it for myself.

Such a circle is not, first of all, experienced through cognition. On the contrary, knowing in this sense is dependent on my world having already been revealed to me. I must live my world before I can know it in this limited way. My world as a whole, on the contrary, is revealed to me by moods. Knowledge directs itself to particular objects and persons in the world, but I cannot know my world as a whole as that which matters to me. This is not because I lack sufficient information, and if I only knew more I could do so. Rather, my world, as that in which I live, and in which equipment and others are intelligible to me, is not available to knowledge at all. If cognition refers to particular objects in the world as present-to-hand (even others), then moods reveal how the world is for me, when for example someone asks 'How are you?' I am always in some mood or other, happy, bored or miserable, and these moods bathe my whole experience of my world in a certain kind of light.[36] What they show to me is that I am always attached to my world in one way or another. In other words, my world always affects me as a whole. I am not just happy, bored or miserable about this or that thing, rather my world as a whole is joyous, boring or miserable. Traditional philosophy, on the contrary, treats moods as merely a subjective colouring which have to be dispensed with if we really want to know what objects are, but this is precisely because it takes categorical Being, as we discussed earlier, to be the only way of Being.[37]

The way my world always affects me, and that I am attached to it before I have made any decision or choice to be so, Heidegger calls 'thrownness' (*Geworfenheit*) (BT: 174). We have already come across this word before, when we thought about how the past colours our understanding of Being, but now we can understand for the first time the source of the weight of tradition.[38] It belongs to Dasein's existence, as such, that it is always delivered over to its world which affects it, and it is this pull or drag of my world which is the ultimate force and power of the domination of the past.[39] It is not just a storehouse of facts which have happened, and which we might read about in books, but belongs to my present as the very fact of my existence – that one is what one is and no other. Such a basic fact of existence (Heidegger calls it 'facticity' (*Faktizität*) to differentiate it from the mere objective facts about something) is not something that I can decide without conditions, but it still something I have decided to be (BT: 174). This means my 'having been', must, in some way, already pre-exist my immediate experience, even though it belongs to it and shapes its peaks and valleys. My cultural background forms my choices and decisions, but not from the outside in a determinate way. I have to be it for it to have any meaning at all. It is this irredeemable fact of my existence (I have not chosen but must choose) which my moods reveal to me, even though most of the time I relate to them in an evasive way.

What moods reveal to me is my world as a whole, my attunement, or lack of it, with my world. But in a mood, my world is not revealed to me as something present-to-hand, an object of theoretical interest, but as an enigma. A mood is what I live, but always as something I find difficult to articulate (sometimes a hand gesture can say more about my mood than anything I say). This does not mean that moods are less than knowledge, or even that objective cognition has anything to say about them. For if the world did not matter to me existentially, then why would I want to know anything specific about it (can one imagine a permanently bored Einstein)? I do not look at the world as a static camera might (or the camera only really looks at the world because it is a piece of equipment being used by me), but first of all I am affected by it and then I look (a great photographer has a way of being affected by the world which others lack). The world is something, which as a whole, matters to me, and about which I am concerned. In what way it matters to me is made manifest by a mood.

Because moods, as the primary way in which I relate to my world, are not to be thought cognitively, then we should not make the mistake of thinking that the second major characteristic of Dasein's Being-in-the-world, 'understanding' (*Verstehen*) must be. Dasein's understanding does not make good what moods lack. It is not a categorical way of relating to the world, but accompanies every mood I have. We remember from the previous chapter that existence is to be understood as possibility.[40] It is not to be thought logically merely as the opposite to necessity, but ontologically the way in which Dasein is. My world is not just disclosed as a collection of facts, but as possibilities. Whatever situation I find myself in, there are always possibilities. It is the understanding which throws itself ahead into these possibilities as 'projection' (*Entwurf*) (BT: 185). This is not like some kind of plan or programme I have in advance and then apply to my experience of the world. Rather, I am already ahead of myself in the possible and understand myself in these terms. This is why Heidegger can say, even if it sounds paradoxical, Dasein is always more than just what it is. As what I am now, I am already what I am not because I have projected myself forward. Of course what I can or cannot do is not limitless. We are not speaking here of an empty abstract freedom, because I, as we have just seen, am thrown into a world which already determines, in a fundamental way, how I can be. On the other hand, I cannot simply abrogate my responsibility for myself, because I still have to take a stand on what I have become and the possibilities revealed there.

Linked to understanding is what Heidegger calls 'interpretation' (*Auslegung*). It is the working out of the possibilities revealed to me by the understanding. Such a 'working out' should again not be confused with knowledge. Interpretation, as Heidegger describes it in section thirty-two, belongs to the ready-to-hand and the referential totality of the environment, and not to the present-to-hand (BT: 188–95). The interpretation of possibilities is pragmatic and not theoretical. Heidegger writes in the *History of the Concept of Time* that when a child asks me, 'What is this thing?' I answer by explaining its purpose and function.[41] Only when I have interpreted it in this way, or have understood the interpretation, is it possible for me to put it into words and define it in the limited way in which traditionally philosophy has tended to grasp the essence of things. Of course, interpreting the purpose and function of something is setting it within the general horizon of intelligibility of my world (in other words, its possibilities). This is why it is very important to get the relation between the understanding and interpretation the right way around. In order to see something as something, the hammer as a tool which hammers in nails for example, I have to 'see' the context (the relational whole) in which the activity of hammering nails would make sense (BT: 186). For me to see something as having a purpose or function, it already has to be part of my background understanding of my world, and this understanding is not at all similar to a cognitive grasp of a particular object.

One way we can make the distinction between interpretation and understanding, on the one hand, and cognition, on the other, more visible is through the fore-structure of interpretation (BT: 191–2). Interpretation is never just a mere looking at something present-to-hand. Rather it looks both backwards and forwards: 'backwards' in the sense that it is shaped by 'facticity', and forwards by possibilities. The analogy here is with reading. I never come to a text presuppositionless. My reading is already shaped by both my prejudices and expectations. We cannot avoid this. Context-free knowledge is an illusion. Even the most abstract way of looking at something hides its own prejudices and expectations, because this belongs essentially to the way Dasein is.[42] Every interpretation supposes an understanding which guides it, but to complain this is a 'vicious circle' is to take logic to be the guide of existence, rather than existence the guide of logic. The problem with traditional metaphysics is that it thinks logic is true precisely because it believes it to be contextless (which it is not), and thus completely distorts the meaning of existence.

What then is the context of logic? Heidegger answers this question in section thirty-three (BT: 195–203). He understands logic as 'assertion' (*Aussage*) which has three meanings (BT: 196–7):

1. 'Pointing out' – the original sense of *logos* as 'letting some thing be seen as itself' which goes back to the way in which Heidegger described phenomenology in section seven (BT: 55–8).
2. Predication' – a narrower meaning of assertion which is only possible because of this prior 'pointing out'.
3. 'Communication' – that which is pointed out is done so in such a manner that it is easily communicable to others.

If we make an assertion about something (to use Heidegger's example, the hammer is too heavy [BT: 197]), then it ceases to be present to us as ready-to-hand, but becomes present-to-hand. When something is present-to-hand, we talk about it as a 'what' which has this or that property, and is therefore no longer part of our involvement with things and our intimacy with others. None the less, this 'what', which we think is the true objective nature of the thing, has its origin in our prior engagement with the world. The hammer is already present to me before it is a subject with predicates. Heidegger describes assertion as a kind of 'stepping back' (BT: 197). When I make judgements about things, I have a restricted and narrow view of them. If my relation to things as present-to-hand has its original source in the ready-to-hand, then this is not true the other way around. The ready-to-hand never descends from the present-to-hand. My everyday involvement with the hammer is not a limitation of my cognitive grasp of something present-to-hand. If it were not already disclosed by the understanding, and then laid out by interpretation, I could not make any assertions about it (this is why the idea of context-free logic is absurd).

We might describe the history of philosophy, at least for Heidegger, as the illegitimate reversal of the relation between ready-to-hand and present-to-hand. It takes what is ontologically prior, our practical and everyday involvement with my world which matters to me, and makes it derivative of the narrow relation of judgement. Why this is so must have, as we have already discussed, had its origin in the way of Being of Dasein. The emphasis on logic as the only truth of things and the world (which the ancient Greek philosophers were perhaps the first to emphasise) is a anxious flight away from the messiness of the world, which is truer, even if it appears meaningless, than any supposedly true statement, with all its rigour and clarity.

One way we can see this is in the phenomenon of language. At the time of writing *Being and Time*, Heidegger is not at all part of what has been called retrospectively the 'linguistic turn' in philosophy, where what is real is merely a projection of language. On the contrary, language is merely a tool through which I express my understanding and interpretation of the world. The 'about which' that language expresses is not itself linguistic. Why logic, in the restricted sense as judgement, becomes so dominant is that its 'about which' is extremely limited and thereby easily communicable because the thing it speaks about is abstracted from the complex web of existential relations which actually give it meaning and which in turn cannot be reduced to any logical statement. There is something bizarre, as a practice, of philosophers pointing to chairs and tables, and asking what they are, because we can only really understand them in relation to a world in which they have a purpose or a function, and this world, as is hopefully becoming clear, is not a 'what' at all.

To think of language as a tool is to think of it pragmatically. What am I doing when I speak? This leads us to the third structure of Dasein's Being-there, which is 'discourse' (*Rede*). When I speak to another, what I say communicates a shared world which is already intelligible. Such a shared world is not in the words themselves, but what the words express. Language has its ontological possibility in Dasein and not the other way around. To be able to listen and speak to someone we must already be with them in some way or another. It is perfectly possible to imagine an animal or a machine speaking words, but if we do not already share a common meaningful world, these words would not really say anything at all.[43] It is because speaking with one another is the essence of language (we must liberate, Heidegger says, grammar from logic [BT: 208]), and not the words spoken, that what is important about language can become listening and being silent. For in this way, I might be more attentive to what is being spoken about (the matter at hand), than just to the words themselves and to the other who is speaking. What happens for the most part, however, is 'idle chatter' (which we shall look at in the next chapter).[44] The fundamental 'about which' which any true conversation concerns itself with gets replaced by the mere definition of words. So, for example, in reading this book (and Heidegger like most philosophers is mistrustful of writing for this very reason), rather than thinking about what is trying to be thought (the question of Being) in your own genuine way, you are only interested in a glossary of definitions which can be repeated in an essay or exam. This is not thinking but merely the transmission of information when no doubt some time in the future no one really knows what was being thought in the first place.

A genuine conversation is a true one. It discloses my world both as involvement with things and intimacy with others. As such, it also discloses who I am, for I am nothing but involvement and intimacy. What we mean by 'truth' here, however, is not the truth of a mere judgement, as when, for example, I say that all bachelors are men. Moods, understanding and language are all linked together by a more fundamental meaning of truth as disclosure, which Heidegger does not really describe in detail until section forty-four of *Being and Time*. This is why, rather than waiting till later, it is better to explain it now.

Truth and Reality
Traditionally we think of truth as agreement. We say that a statement is true because it agrees with a state of affairs in the world. I say, 'It is raining,' and when you look out of the window it really is raining, so my statement is true. Like with most things which appear obvious, the more we investigate them the less simple they are. Heidegger's approach to the problem of truth in this section is twofold, and it mirrors the method of *Being and Time* as a whole. One part is historical, to remind us that this common sense view of truth comes from a tradition, which in fact has a much more ambiguous and complex understanding of truth; and the other is phenomenological, which attempts to describe the experience of truth as disclosure, and thereby loosen the assumptions and prejudices of this tradition.

As Heidegger remarks at the very start of this section the question of truth and being have always gone together in philosophy (BT: 256). Originally, their association was thought through disclosure (which it should not surprise us Heidegger wants to retrieve), but this insight was overlaid by the logical conception of truth, whose first formulation is to be found in Aristotle (though, as always with the case of Aristotle for Heidegger, what he himself begins becomes watered down as it trickles through philosophical history). It is this logical conception which is the basis of truth as agreement. Yet the more we think about agreement, the more puzzling it seems. Although the existence of the statement is obvious enough and the object it is supposed to agree with, what is it that allows them to agree with one another? Is it something in the statement, or in the object itself? But if they are two different kinds of beings (nobody thinks that a statement is the same as a thing), what allows them to agree at all?

Heidegger's response to these questions is neither to find a better theory of correspondence, nor even to dismiss this theory, but to show that this conception must have its basis in a more fundamental experience of truth. Our previous discussion of the sections on understanding, interpretation and assertion should already make this dependence clear to us. Logical statements (whether true or false) are assertions and they, as we have already seen, are dependent upon a prior uncovering of things in the world, their original disclosure, whose source is the Being of Dasein.

Heidegger unpacks the hidden ontology of the traditional conception of truth through a phenomenological example (BT: 260–1). Let us imagine someone has their back turned to the wall and they make the assertion, 'The picture on the wall is crooked.' At what point does this assertion become true? Does not the truth happen when they turn around and see that the picture really is crooked? What Heidegger stresses is that truth happens not in the statement nor even in the head of the person who utters it, but when the picture reveals itself as it is to the person who is standing there. If the picture did not show or manifest itself to me, then how could I say anything about it at all? The possibility of the statement being true or false, in the logical sense, therefore, is dependent on the phenomenological (in the way Heidegger describes it in section seven) experience of uncovering (*Entdeckend*). This uncovering, in turn, however, is only possible because the world as such is disclosed to me. Truth is not, first of all, a description of statements, but a way of Being in the world. If things were not present to me in my world, then I would not be able to make statements about them. This originally, Heidegger asserts, is how the Greeks understood the phenomenon of truth, before it was overlaid by its logical conception. The Greek word for truth, *aletheia*, literally means 'unforgetting', 'un-concealing', or 'unhiddenness' (BT: 262).[45]

If truth is a way of Being-in-the-world, then it can only belong to a being who has a world. The only being which has a world is Dasein. That I can make judgements and assertions about things in the world must mean that they are 'there' in some way or other. That they are 'there', however, is dependent on a more primordial 'there' which is the region of disclosure. Such a 'space', as we have already seen, is not itself a being. It is neither present-to-hand, nor ready-to-hand, but is the world in which things are intelligible. Things are present to me because they are meaningful, but they are only meaningful because they have their place within the overall context of my world. This is why Heidegger can write that Dasein exists in the truth (BT: 263). Does this not sound dangerously like relativism? Things are only true because we experience them so? To answer this question we must turn back briefly to the section that immediately precedes this one, 'Dasein, Worldhood and Reality' (BT: 244–56).

One of the oldest questions of philosophy is whether the world exists or not. Which philosophy student has not been seduced by Descartes' thought experiment that the world might be nothing but a dream? How can we respond to this question? Certainly not by attempting to prove the world does exist. Some philosophical questions can only be answered by showing they are badly formulated, rather than by coming up with an alternative answer. The possibility of imagining the world to be fiction has its source in a metaphysics which is ontologically false. I can only imagine myself separate from the world, if my only relation to it is representational, but it is precisely such a conception which is prejudicial. Why must I conceive of my Being in this way? Am I not, as Heidegger has shown us, already in the world, and does not the possibility of even coming up with such absurd philosophical fantasies have its basis there?

Heidegger's response to this problem means that it is difficult to place him in the split between realism and idealism which has characterised philosophy since Descartes, and around which it seems permanently to oscillate (though he does say there is more truth to idealism than realism [BT: 251]). The world is not a representation, but nor is it external to me as the aggregate of natural things. What is common to idealism and realism is that they both lack a proper ontological understanding of the world. I am not an element within the world, but nor is it apart from me. On the contrary, there is no such thing as the world, if we think of it as a being (whether this being is real or ideal). The world, rather, is a way of Being of Dasein. It is not a substance at all, but a verb. Only out of this way of Being can the question of reality of the world itself arise, but it immediately distorts how Dasein actually exists in a world. Both realism and idealism (even if their solutions might be very different) treat Dasein and the world as though they were something present-to-hand, which then, in a second moment, have to be stuck back together again after being separated. Heidegger is not about to provide a solution to this age-old problem. Rather, he shows that such issues are absurd because of the way the problem is formulated. I am already in a world. I am my world. The world is me. Ontologically speaking, the world and I are inseparable. Not because the world and I are the same thing, but because Being-in-the-world is what it means to be the kind of being I am, and it is only through such an understanding that any beings are accessible at all

Anxiety, Death and Guilt

What I cannot face is the meaninglessness of my life. I will die and do so alone. What does it matter to the community of the human race that I have died? Perhaps my friends and family might remember me, but they too will die. So I need, while I live, to forget my death. I must fill this meaninglessness with significance. I fall back into the world and busy myself with things and others. I speak. Each moment of speech is the irruption of meaning into world. It is as though the world begins again with my birth. In itself, however, this redemption is a false one. For what the world promises me, it also takes away. Rather than a true dialogue with things and others (or more precisely only with others, since it is only through them that I can have an authentic relation with things), I am surrounded by anonymous discourse which comes from nowhere. I am addressed constantly. My life is saturated by signs (we live in a world of communication), but I cannot speak to them. I only consume them. How do I escape this whirlwind? By facing what I want to avoid: the meaninglessness of my life.

The importance of anxiety and death to Heidegger's analysis is that they are not morbid phenomena. They are, in fact, what make us truly human as opposed to mere animals. So far, he argues, we have only described Dasein's inauthentic existence. Now we have to show what it means to be authentic. This is not because *Being and Time* is some kind of philosophical life style book (though philosophy ought to affect how we lives our lives), but it does have important methodological reasons. We remember from the very beginning that Heidegger's question is the meaning of Being in general and not just the Being of Dasein. The analytic of Dasein is merely a means to end. It is because Dasein is the only being whose Being is an issue for it that it is the clue to the meaning of Being in general. Yet if such a question is the key to the meaning of Being, how does Dasein's Being become an issue for it? My Being certainly is not a question for me if I am absorbed in the world. It can only be so if I break with its fascination and temptation. There must be a life condition for the possibility of philosophy and the analysis of anxiety and death is the description of why something like the writing of *Being and Time* could have happened at all and even that you might be interested in reading it. This is not just a biological fact (dogs and stones cannot read), but an existential or interpretative one. Why is it that you are interested in the meaning of your life as a whole? And of course there are others who are not, who just want to be absorbed into the world as we all are to some extent and have to be.

This question brings us to another methodological issue for Heidegger and one that is more pertinent to the writing of *Being and Time*. How is it possible to grasp Dasein's Being as whole, rather than as fragmented into different possibilities and projects? Again, the reason that Heidegger wants to view Dasein's Being as whole has to do with the overall question of *Being and Time*, which is the meaning of Being in general. By being able to grasp Dasein as whole, we will also be able to see the ultimate horizon of its Being. This horizon is time, which is the fundamental topic of the second division, and which will be explained in the final part of the book. Of course, we have been talking about time all along, but only then will it become vivid to us. This part will be divided into three sections: the first will examine falling and anxiety; the second, death; and the last guilt and resoluteness. The material here straddles the first and second divisions of *Being and Time*, and covers what we left out in the previous part. It moves from inauthenticity to authenticity, because it is only the latter which allows us to grasp the deep temporal structure of human existence and, since it is only we who discourse about Being, why it too can only be spoken about through time.

Falling and Anxiety

In the previous part, we jumped over Heidegger's description of the everyday experience of Being-in-the-world, so as to explain the existential meaning of truth, because I believed it sat better with the order of explanation of *Being and Time*. Now, however, we have to return to this experience, otherwise it will not be clear to us what it is that anxiety, so to speak, goes against, and in so doing how it reveals the structure of Dasein's Being, which Heidegger calls 'care' (*Sorge*).

Dasein is in the world through moods, understanding and language, but how are these lived in the everyday world? We remember from the previous part that for Heidegger what is essential in language is not the words spoken but what is spoken about. In speaking to others (and even to ourselves) what matters is what it is we are talking about which reveals something about our world. This interpretive power of language, as opposed to the mere fact of words, Heidegger calls 'discourse' (*Rede*). Do we really, however, talk this way for the most part? Would it not be truer to say that on the whole we simply talk, and what it is we are talking about does not really matter at all? When I speak to people I meet on the street or at work, I am mostly just passing the time of day. If you were to ask me what it was we spoke about, I really would not be able to tell you, or if I did, I would say it was not important. This is not to say I do not have genuine conversations, but they are rare in comparison.

The common and everyday way that we talk together Heidegger describes in section thirty-five as 'idle chatter' (*Gerede*) and it is the opposite of discourse (BT: 211–14). Such chatter is the basis of my everyday involvement with others. It is the medium which glues us together. We traffic together through words which are no longer about anything at all and it is because of them we end up interpreting ourselves as having the same interests and desires as everyone else. This is so because no one really knows any more what these words are about. It is as though the endless chatter from all the different media has completely blocked out any sense of what might or might not be important. Such is the source of the feeling we have that, despite the fact we have more information than perhaps any other generation we actually know less. This also explains the other phenomenon of every-day absorption in the world which Heidegger describes as 'curiosity' (*Neugier*), in section thirty-six (BT: 214–17), because what is talked and written about no longer has any basis in something significant. The public world is one of endless curiosity, because there is nothing to stop the gaze. Every experience is an equal to any other experience, because no experience is sufficiently important in itself. Reality becomes a spectacle of consumption. Rather than being directly involved with things and intimate with others, I distance myself from them (curiosity is an exaggerated form of 'de-severance')[46] and simply devour them up from afar. It is not that they matter to me, because it is unlikely that I really know them at all and I certainly do not have any serious engagement with them. All I see is their image which begins to take over every aspect of my reality, so that even in my conversations with others all I talk about is the image.

If idle chatter and curiosity are the everyday forms of discourse and understanding, then the last form, 'ambiguity' (*Zweideutigkeit*) is not a negative corollary of moods (BT: 217–19). This is because moods (whether negative or positive) are always revelatory for Heidegger. They tell me something about the world in which I exist. This is why talking, when it is not serious, is a fleeing away from what moods reveal. Ambiguity is not a mood, but a confusion of under-standing or interpretation. The spectacle is so effervescent that I no longer know what is important or not. What is spoken about, dis-cussed and communicated is so noisy that I can no longer discern what is worth listening to. Because I cannot make out what is worth seeing, listening or doing, then I end up following what everyone else is seeing, listening to and doing. Yet when I ask someone why they are looking at, listening to and doing this, they equally have no more reason to do so than I have. What is ambiguous about this phenome-non is that its source is Being with others, but at the same time this type of relation to others is what prevents me from having an authen-tic relation to them.

We might say, however, that this ambiguity extends over the whole of the everyday. It is very important we do not misunderstand this description as a censure, otherwise Heidegger will just end up sound-ing like a reactionary conservative of the worst kind (there is no doubt some think he is so). This is not an ontic description of an age gone bad, but an ontological investigation of the kind of being which Dasein is. The everyday is not something, therefore, we should get rid of, or even could do so, but belongs to what it is to be Dasein. It is therefore a positive ontological phenomenon (other beings can never experience the everyday). Two important consequences follow from this: one, that Heidegger is attempting to save the everyday in *Being and Time* against traditional metaphysics which tends to see it as something which has to be transcended in order to reach true knowledge; and two, that the authentic relationship to things and others in the world must have its source in the everyday, and not the other way around. In other words, Heidegger is not seeking to get beyond the everyday, but to show how the everyday is already involved, because of the way which Dasein is, in what cannot be experienced as the everyday. We can already see this, for example, in Heidegger's description of curiosity. If we were not curious at all, then there could not be any possible involvement with things or intimacy with others. Even cognition, which is a particular way of seeing, has its basis in everyday curiosity (BT: 215). Of course, if we fail to understand the ontological roots of curiosity in Dasein's Being, then it can become the endless and meaningless form which Heidegger describes.

Dasein's occupation by rather than in the everyday Heidegger calls, in section thirty-eight, 'falling' (*Verfallen*) (BT: 219–24). It belongs to the way that Dasein is that it is wholly and completely absorbed, distracted and bemused by the world. The 'in' of 'inauthenticity' should, therefore, not be understood negatively. Dasein is not itself, when it has 'fallen' into the world. Quite the contrary, this is just how it is. But in so being, the phenomenon of the world remains invisible to it. Not the world, as a collection of events and happenings, which of course it is obsessed and consumed by precisely because it has so fallen, but the worldhood of the world, what makes it possible, as part of its own Being, that there is a world for it to be absorbed by in the first place. Here for the first time we can begin to understand the importance of the mood of anxiety for Heidegger (again remembering it is always moods which reveal the world as a whole to us). It makes visible what is invisible in fallenness.

Heidegger says that what is lacking in our everyday Being-in-the-world is a 'ground to stand on' (BT: 168). We might be tempted, especially because of Heidegger's own political decisions, to interpret such a lack as part of the ideology of 'blood and soil', but we would be quite wrong to do so.[47] Yes, Heidegger will be searching, in his description of authenticity, for a ground for Dasein's Being, but what we will discover, and this is what is so strange and unsettling, is that this ground is in fact nothing. We therefore have to distinguish between the groundlessness of everyday existence in which Dasein, like a leaf in the wind, is blown in this direction and that, and the experience of nothingness which is genuine to anxiety. It is because at bottom Dasein's Being is nothing, that its total absorption in any world is ontologically impossible. Ontically, the everyday is first, but ontologically it is the nothing which is fundamental. The nothing is what makes any world possible. It is, so to speak, the 'space' (existentially understood) which it occupies, but it is also at the same time what makes any Dasein singular, because the origin of this nothing is its own Being. This means that no Dasein is wholly synonymous with the particular cultural world in which it lives. The difference between a world (Japanese, English and so on), and the worldhood of the world is precisely this nothing, and it is this which individuates Dasein (the nothing is not a definition of Dasein, but a way of Being which is specific to Dasein). The fact that existence is always 'mine', is only because at the heart of my existence there is nothing (in other words, I am not reducible to any predicate which is said of me).[48]

This all sounds very peculiar at the moment, but every creative philosopher, precisely because he has to seek out a problem in a new way to make us think, pushes at the limits of what any language, at a particular point in historical time, can communicate. Who does not struggle with Aristotle and Kant even today? A commentary would be useless if it pretended philosophy were simple and could be easily digested. To seek to do so would be even more bizarre in relation to Heidegger, for it would be to reduce his work to idle chatter, curiosity and ambiguity. None the less, it is my endeavour in this part to explain what this nothing means, and we shall begin to do so with the mood of anxiety which is described by Heidegger in section forty (BT: 228–35).

Anxiety is a fundamental mood which reveals the worldhood of the world to us, but it does so first of all negatively. For we must remember that Heidegger has only just described to us what everyday

Being-in-the-world is. Whatever it is that anxiety reveals must be what everyday existence is in flight from. What it flees from the phenomenologist must follow. What Dasein is in flight from, though it might not know this itself, is itself. But what is this 'itself'? Is it like a thing in the world, or a person? What am I fleeing, when I say that I am fleeing myself? Heidegger would respond that I am trying to escape my uniqueness or singularity. I want to be defined like a thing, or live like other people. Before we, however, try to understand what this self might be which I am trying to avoid, I have to think of the status of this mood itself. Here Heidegger distinguishes fear from anxiety. Fear, which he described previously, is always fear of something in the world which threatens my existence (BT: 179–82). Anxiety, on the contrary, has no object. I am not anxious about this thing or that person in my world, but my world as such. It is to get away from this anxiety about my existence that I flee from the question of myself and absorb myself in the world. Precisely because it is not this or that which I am anxious about, the first quality of the mood of anxiety is indefiniteness (BT: 231). It is the indefinite object of anxiety which fills me with horror such that I shrink away from it and busy myself with the world.

What the mood of anxiety reveals, if I were to follow it, is that my world which I occupy myself with (the world of the ready and present-to-hand) rests on nothing. What conceals the worldhood of the world is the things and people I relate to, and with which and whom I busy my time. All this coming and going conceals the ontological basis of my world, but occasionally and perhaps without premeditation, anxiety can strip all this way, dissolving them into a fog of nothingness, such that for a moment my world as a whole is revealed. Worldhood, as opposed to a world, cannot itself be something, either present or ready-to-hand. This is why Heidegger says that it comes from 'nowhere' and is 'nothing' (BT: 231). What is ontologically nothing, however, is not the same as what is ontically nothing. When I say that something is not, I just mean it does not exist. But when Heidegger says Dasein exists ontologically as nothing, then he does not mean just that it does not exist. Rather, we have to understand Being as nothing positively. It is not an assertion about things but a way of Being. Dasein is nothing if we understand 'is' existentially and not categorically. It is nothing because it is not a thing, and when we say the worldhood of the world is nothing this is because the onto-logical origin of any particular ontic world is the Being of Dasein whose Being is neither present nor ready-to-hand. Metaphysics fails, as we have seen, because it wants to define Dasein as special kind of thing, but it is literally 'no-thing' at all.

This is why we can also think of the nothing in terms of possibili-ties, because the possible is how we understand the Being of Dasein. When I am absorbed in the world, I worry about this or that possi-bility. Am I a good enough philosophy teacher or student and so on? But this is not what I am anxious about. Just as I am not anxious about this or that thing or person in the world, so too am I not anxious about any specific possibility. On the contrary, what makes me anxious is the being possible as such. Every possibility exists, which I could actualise or not, in the sea of the possible which is nothing. This is not nihilism, because such an attitude exists in relation to specific values which belong to particular world. Nihilism, therefore, is one way of being occupied by a world, of fleeing from the nothing which you are. Anxiety, instead, throws me back to myself not so I should be this or that person, but so that I should relate to my possibilities as my own, and I can only do so from out of the nothingness which is at the heart of my existence. Every time I say here there is something which indi-viduates me (my spectacular wit, for example), then I am lying, for what I utter are common properties. What individuates me is nothing. The greatest temptation is to fill this nothing with something, but it is a temptation which belongs to Dasein because it is nothing. Authenticity for Heidegger is not being this or that person, actualis-ing this or that possibility, rather it is facing the nothingness which is at the heart of your existence as nothing and holding fast to it. The status of this nothing will become clearer when we examine the following sections on death, the call of conscience and guilt.

Being towards Death

The importance of death for Heidegger is that it reveals, in the sharpest way possible, the particular distinctive nature of the Being of Dasein. But we might think, before we arrive at the first chapter of division two of *Being and Time*, that we have already achieved this insight. Does not Heidegger tell us after the description of anxiety that we now understand the Being of Dasein through the unified structure of care? Ahead of advancing into the detail of Heidegger's investigation of death, let us ask ourselves, therefore, what this structure is, and why he still felt it necessary to write the second division of *Being and Time*, even though the Being of Dasein seems now fully revealed.

Heidegger tells us in section forty-one that Dasein's Being should be grasped as a totality (BT: 235). It is this totality which is revealed by anxiety. I am anxious about my Being as a whole and not something in the world. But what is this whole? Heidegger typifies it by the three directions of Dasein's Being. One is towards being thrown into the world (facticity); the other is towards my possibilities (existence); and both demonstrate that I always exist alongside other beings within the world (fallenness or falling). These three together make up what Heidegger calls 'care' which he glosses as follows: 'The Being of Dasein means ahead-of-itself-Being-already in-(the world) as Being-alongside (entities encountered within-the-world)' (BT: 237). All this sounds very abstract at the moment and it reads merely as a definition of Dasein's Being rather than something it has to accomplish. It is not until we come to the chapters on time in division two (and which we will discuss in the next part) that we get any real understanding of what this unity might be. Even before we get there, however, there is a more immediate problem. For, as Heidegger begins the chapter on death, does it not belong to the way which Dasein is that it cannot be a whole because it always dies? Either I am alive, and therefore not complete, since there is something ahead of me, or I am dead, but then there is nothing there to experience it.

Why should this be such a problem for Heidegger? We must remember the aim of his book from the very beginning is to reawaken the question of the meaning of Being in general. The only being whose Being is an issue for it is Dasein, but if I cannot grasp my Being as a whole (not just as a disconnected series of events or happenings), then how can my Being be an issue for me? If it cannot, then the question of Being is everything Heidegger says it has become at the beginning of *Being and Time*, empty, trivial and indefinable. Is the language of totality, whole and unity, however, appropriate to Dasein as a finite being? In what sense can my life be a whole, when it always ends in death? Heidegger is going to answer this question, as he tends to do, in a roundabout way. He is, first of all, going to suggest that a certain way of speaking about a whole is not suitable to Dasein, but if we understand existentially, then it is.

When we talk about the end or totality of Dasein, then we are not speaking about it in the same way we might speak about something present-to-hand as having an objective limit. Death is not an end in this way. Of course, we have a tendency to think of death as though it were. We might imagine our lives like a line which begins with our birth and ends with our death, but it is exactly for this reason that we end up with the paradox that Dasein either is and is incomplete, or is not and complete. If I exist, then I am still 'not-yet', because there are possibilities ahead of me, or there are no more possibilities, but in that case I am dead. How can I experience my whole life and still be alive? We might think, Heidegger offers in section forty-seven, that we can answer this dilemma through the death of others (BT: 281–5). I cannot experience my own death, but I can experience theirs. But in death is not the other just a corpse and therefore a thing? I might reply that the deceased is not just a thing, otherwise why would we have funeral rites? But even then do I really experience the death of the other? Is not the death of the other part of my life, because they were someone who mattered to me, rather then theirs? I no more experience the transition from life to death through the other than I do in my own life. This brings Heidegger to an important conclusion (one which is really jumping ahead of his argument) that we have to face death alone: 'Dying is something that every Dasein itself must take upon itself at the time' (BT: 284).

I say Heidegger might have got ahead of himself here, because it could appear that he means Dasein has to die alone, which is manifestly absurd since many people do not do so. Such criticism, however, profoundly misunderstands the significance of death in *Being and Time*. It is primarily concerned with death as a possibility and not as an actuality. Interest in the latter is how everyday existence avoids its existential significance. Before Heidegger comes to this, however, he still wants sharply to distinguish, in section forty-eight, the end of Dasein from other ways in which we might speak about ends (BT: 285–90). He spends so much time going through these distinctions because we continually fail to understand Dasein's Being as existence, and confuse it with the Being of things which we encounter in the world (a confusion whose source, as we know, is Dasein itself as fallenness).

As long as I exist, I exist in the possible, in the 'not-yet', because there are still things to do. This not yet is not a lack which is then filled to make Dasein complete. This is to imagine Dasein as composite to which something needs to be added in order to make it whole. But I am what I am because of my 'not-yets', not despite them. Our confusion arises here because we are thinking of Dasein as something present-to-hand which is missing some external part which only needs to be added to it in order for it to be whole, in the way, to use Heidegger's example, we might think that a debt is outstanding until it is paid off (BT: 286). But my end, my death, is not outstanding in this way. Perhaps the more appropriate example, Heidegger adds, is that of the fruit whose 'not yet ripeness' belongs to what it is, rather than something which is appended to it from the outside (BT: 287–8). But even this similarity is only superficial. For the ripeness of the fruit completes it. It is, to use the more Aristotelian language, the actualisation of its potentiality, its final cause. Death is not my final cause. Does my death fulfil my purpose? Is not Heidegger right to suggest that most people die unfulfilled (BT: 288)?

The difference between death as a 'not-yet' of Dasein, and these other processes, whether of a sum which is added to, or a course which is completed or not, is that the latter is always a case of actualisation, whereas the former always remains open as a possibility. The debt is actually paid off or not, the fruit actually ripens or it does not. But my death, which has not happened yet, is not experienced by me as an actuality, but as a permanent possibility. Of course, as Heidegger will later point out, my death can be treated as an actuality, but only from the outside and not by me, because it is the very possibility of my impossibility. I think of it as an actuality because I see it as a fact which happens externally. Heidegger does not deny this. I die just like everything else does. But I do not just die; I can also live my death. I, already whilst I am alive, can have a relation to my death. But this death is now not an actuality, but a possibility. I am aware that at any moment it is possible I can die. The authentic relation to death is the relation to this possibility and not to its actuality.

The difference between death as an actuality (true of all things, even the universe) and death as a possibility is what Heidegger makes explicit by the phrase, 'Being-towards-death' (*Sein-zum-Tode*) which he distinguishes from 'Being-at-an-end' (BT: 289). Death, in the first case, is not something which happens to me at the end of my life, rather it is that towards which I am already directed at the very instant of my birth, because it is always possible at any moment of my life. This is not to deny, as Heidegger remarks in the following section forty-nine, that there cannot be other kinds of investigation of death (such as in biology or anthropology), but they always treat death as a fact, whereas it is only death as a possibility which reveals the unique Being of Dasein (BT: 291–3).

Let us look more deeply at what Heidegger means by death as a possibility in section fifty (BT: 293–6). It is not enough to say death is impending, for there are many possibilities, as Heidegger indicates, which are so, like a nearing storm or waiting for a friend. What is unique about the possibility of death is that it throws Dasein back upon its own possibility of Being. This is because, unlike any other possibility, it is the one possibility which strips me of all others. This is what Heidegger means when he says death is the 'possibility of the absolute impossibility of Dasein' (BT: 294).[49] As such, it discloses to Dasein the whole of its Being as possible. For in being aware of my impending death (and I am so through the mood of anxiety and not cognitively), all my other possibilities, my relations to things and others, are stripped away. I understand that everything which they stand upon is fragile and transitory, for I could die at any moment, and all of this would disappear. This is precisely why the everyday relation to death attempts to avoid this insight and it does so by transforming death into an actuality. It is thought of as an event in the world, whether it concerns one death or many; someone close, or strangers far away. As Heidegger says in section fifty-one, there is a minimal recognition of death in this opinion, but it pushes death away as a possibility which might happen to me (BT: 296–9). I know that I will die, but this is an anonymous fact which happens to everyone (and in this way to no one). I think of death as an actuality which occurs at the end of my life, and not as an impending possibility which can happen at any moment. I am no longer anxious about my death as a future possibility which reveals my life as a whole, but fear death as an event and wonder how I might avoid it or prolong my life, even though this life might be perfectly meaningless; or, if I have the courage, even though I am meant to be completely indifferent to it.

Everyone knows they will die, but such certainty avoids the existential import of Being-towards-death. We say this to ourselves so we do not have to face our own death as a possibility. It is just one more fact of life. We can be certain about the empirical fact of death, but this is not the same as being certain about the possibility of our own death. True, we know we will die, but this should not be confused with some kind of existential composure. On the contrary, existentially speaking, death is always uncertain, because as Heidegger writes, it is 'possible at any moment' (BT: 258). Empirically certain, existentially uncertain, death reveals the precarious nature of my life. It is this transience which is covered over by my everyday occupations. I fill in time so as to conceal the nothingness which lies at its heart. I imagine my existence as something permanent, substantial, like a thing. It is not death as a fact which is terrifying, because everything dies and there is even something consoling about that thought. What is far more disturbing is the relation between life and death in a life which understands it can end at any moment and whose future, therefore, is always held out into its own disappearance. Such a recognition, which is a disclosure of my whole life, affects every one of my possibilities now. In terms of their content, they might not be any different. I might still be a teacher of philosophy, but how I relate to this content will be very different indeed.

What such a different relation might be is the topic of the next section in the description of the authentic attitude towards death, but it is also the subject of the next part, on the call of conscience, guilt and resoluteness (BT: 304–11). If the pull of everyday life is so powerful, how is it possible to have an authentic regard for our own death as a permanent possibility which cannot be avoided? Just as was the case in anxiety, we have to look at what it is Dasein is fleeing away from when it avoids understanding its own death. It is not death as such, as we have just seen, since everyone recognises its inevitability, but the possibility of death. An authentic attitude towards death, therefore, understands it as a possibility, but in so doing its whole relation to its life is completely transformed.

Usually we think of possibility in terms of the primacy of actuality. Something is possible because it can be actualised and not the other way around. In Heidegger's language, it is either ready or present-to-hand. But death is not a possibility in this way. Being-towards-death is not about actualising death as a possibility, otherwise suicide would be the most authentic decision in the face of death. It is not about morbidly wondering about how my death might happen, but facing up to its permanent possibility, and how such a constant threat affects my life as a whole. At this point in his analysis, Heidegger distinguishes between 'expectation' (*Erwarten*) and 'anticipation' (*Vorlaufen*) (BT: 306). When I expect something, I am imagining its realisation. When I anticipate, on the other hand, I am still holding open its possibility. In German, *Vorlaufen* literally means 'running ahead'. I do not run ahead into death by actualising it, but by understanding the possibility of death as that which is the most imminent possibility of my life. There is nothing to actualise in this vision, because death, as we have seen, is the possibility of impossibility, and therefore is unlike any other.

It is not sufficient, however, to say I can anticipate my own death as a possibility for me to be authentic. There has to be a disclosure. In this vision, I see I am lost in the They. Only now do I realise what Heidegger means when he says every Dasein must die alone. What my anticipation of my death as a possibility reveals to me is my life. Not life in general, but the life I am living now. As I sit here wasting my time, wondering why my life is going nowhere, it is possible, through anxiety, that I can suddenly anticipate my own death. What if I were to die now watching this rubbish on television; would I really have lived a life worth living? To give meaning to our life is to anticipate our own death. This is what Heidegger means by 'freedom' (BT: 311). It is not the arbitrary choice of any possibility (and as thrown beings arbitrary choices are a fiction), but choosing who you already are, but this time as your own choice and not just because others have chosen for you. None of this is a cry for individualism, since what it means to be you is to be intimately connected to things and others (I am only me because of them, and not despite them), but it is to have a 'free' relation to them rather than a trapped one.

The Call of Conscience, Guilt and Resoluteness

Heidegger says at the end of the chapter on death that he has described what it would mean to be authentic, but not how anyone might achieve it (BT: 311). The next part, and the sections which follow, are meant to answer this question. We now know that for the most part Dasein exists as They exist. Being a self, therefore, is not a metaphysical construction, a property of a thing called Dasein, but an achievement and accomplishment. But how actually do I carry it through when the temptation to absorb and involve myself in the everyday world is so powerful? There must be, Heidegger says, something externally which forces Dasein out of its self-satisfaction and comfort in the world. He labels it the 'call of conscience' (*Ruf des Gewissens*). As we shall see this 'outside' is in fact internal to Dasein. It calls to itself out of the gravitational pull of the They. What this call bears witness to is Dasein's guilt, and in recognising it Dasein is resolute. 'Call of conscience', 'guilt', 'resoluteness', all this sounds very theological, but as elsewhere in *Being and Time*, Heidegger is adamant this is an ontological analysis and presupposes no faith or belief in God. What we have to do is understand these expressions on their own terms and judge if they are phenomenologically accurate. Let us first examine, therefore, what Heidegger means by the call of conscience in the following three sections (BT: 315–25).

The call of conscience belongs to discourse. It, as we have already seen, is the way in which Dasein is disclosed to itself. It belongs to the understanding, and the understanding to the possibilities of Dasein.[50] Because understanding is discourse, it is not a theoretical judgement about possibilities, but a listening or hearing. Of course, what Heidegger means by listening or hearing here is not empirical, but an ontological disclosure. For it to be possible for me to break out of the restricted possibilities which are given to me by the They, I must be able to 'hear' the possibility of Being myself. What I am responding to is the call of conscience. Such a call does not have any information. Nor does it communicate anything particular to me. On the contrary, in relation to the noise of the everyday world, it is silent. It is not a vocal call at all, but an awakening of myself from out of the bewitchment of the world.

If the call of conscience belongs to discourse, then there must be something it discloses. What is the subject of the call of conscience? The subject is Dasein who is called to be a self as a way of Being. Being a self, therefore, is a vocation, but it is only so because I can be called to it. Dasein is the caller and the called. We should not confuse this call out of ourselves to ourselves (the first self being the 'they-self' and the second, the authentic self), as a morbid introspection. Such an obsession with ourselves is just one more vivid expression of the domination of the They. On the contrary, the call to be ourselves is the recognition of ourselves as Being-in-the-world. What the call calls me to be, from within myself, is to own my possibilities rather than to live them through the vicarious imprimatur of the They. Even with this change of attitude, I am still occupied with the business of the world through my everyday relations to things and others. What has changed is only how I relate to them. Rather than they owning me, I own them. Such an owning is not a possessing, but freeing them to be what they are. A hammer is free to be a hammer because I release it for this possibility. And I care for others only to the extent that I free them for their own possibilities rather than take them over.

Neither the caller nor what is called is anything distinct or definite. I am not called to be or do anything. Such definite possibilities are precisely how the They calls. Rather I am appealed to silently from within myself out of my lostness in the world. It is the very indistinctness and indefiniteness of this call which breaks through the 'idle chatter'. If the call, as Heidegger writes, 'comes from out of me and beyond me', then I should not interpret this as a voice which speaks to me from outside (the voice of God, for example) (BT: 320). Rather it 'speaks' from the very depths of Dasein's Being. It marks Dasein's unease with himself (him 'not being at home' with himself which Heidegger described in anxiety). Such a disquiet is not psychological but ontological. It belongs to the very structure of Dasein's Being that he is not at home, no matter how hard he tries to be so, in the world.

Such 'not being at home' which belongs essentially to Dasein's Being, is what Heidegger means by guilt in section fifty-eight (BT: 325–35). In German, guilt (*Schuld*) also means 'debt'. Being in debt has a notion of being delivered over to something, as when I say I am in debt to someone. The debt Heidegger is referring to here is ontological. Dasein's debt to his Being, so to speak, is its thrownness. I am delivered over to an existence whose origin I cannot get back behind. In this way, I am responsible, in being myself, for what is 'not me'. My indebtedness (which is another way of speaking about my facticity) is revealed to me by anxiety, but what is disclosed here is understood as a possibility. Thus, what I am is not behind but before me. I am not only responsible for my existence as what I have 'not yet' become, but what I have been as ahead of me. Being guilty, in this sense, for Heidegger, is being responsible for a double nothingness which lies at the heart of my existence, or as he describes it, 'Being the null basis of a nullity' (BT: 329).[51] I am not responsible for what is 'not me' and what is 'not yet', thrownness and projection. It is exactly this nothingness which is covered over by my occupation by the everyday world, such that I understand myself only in terms of the possibilities which are given to me as fixed and permanent, and not as the null ground of these possibilities as the 'not' of thrown projection.

Although our everyday experiences must be the guide for our ontological analysis they should not determine it. Ordinarily, Heidegger points out in section fifty-nine, conscience is understood as the weighing up of good and bad actions or intentions (BT: 335–41).[52] Being guilty, in this case, happens after the deed. This is to reverse the correct temporality of Dasein's Being. What is behind me is always before me. My Being is not a description of a state of affairs, but a project I have to perform (or fail to perform). Such a 'performance' has its basis in my own ability to be, and makes no judgement about this or that particular possibility as being good or bad.

This is why it is important we do not understand this nullity or nothingness at the heart of Dasein's existence ontically. It is not because Dasein lacks some concrete possibility that it is guilty. Rather, only because ontologically speaking the basis of its Being is nothing can it have any concrete possibilities at all. Only if Dasein were all possibilities in the world would nothingness not be at the heart of existence (in other words, if it were God). We know, however, that in choosing this or that possibility all other possibilities are not possible. What the call of conscience appeals to is Dasein's recognition of its own finitude ('wanting to have a conscience'); what it really means to exist as a mortal being who understands it is mortal. Such an understanding, which is a particular kind of authentic possibility, Heidegger calls, in section sixty, 'resoluteness' (*Entschlossenheit*), whose German intentionally recalls disclosure (*Erschlossenheit*) (BT: 341–8).

Being resolute, I am open to the disclosure of my Being and I hold onto myself in this openness. Only out of this resoluteness can there be an authentic relation to things (concern) and others (solicitude). Again, resoluteness must be a possibility which is projected ahead of ourselves. Such a projection, Heidegger calls a 'resolution' or 'decision' (*Entschluß*) (BT: 345). Most of the time we do not make a decision about our lives, but just drift along, thinking and doing what others think and do. Our Being only becomes an issue for us when we do make a stand upon who we are. This does not have to change what we are, and it certainly does not mean we cut ourselves off from the world, but it does change how we relate to what we are. It transforms our reality from a mere succession of barely distinguishable events and occurrences, in which we are lost in our daily habits and rituals, into a 'situation' (BT: 346). I am not resolute because there are situations (dangerous, exciting or otherwise), but because I am resolute there are situations. Rather than accepting my possibilities as fixed (as though they were actualities), I face them as possibilities and as my own. We might get confused about resoluteness and think it is about being certain, but I think it is quite the opposite. It is about being absolutely unsure about our existence and this is what it means to live in the possible, rather than the actual.

The purpose of the first and second chapters of division two of *Being and Time* is to show that Dasein's Being as a whole can be understood and it is possible for an individual Dasein to do so. Heidegger believes he has demonstrated this by showing that authentic existence is possible. What is still not clear, however, is how this way of Being of Dasein is a clue to the meaning of Being in general, which we know is the general aim of the book. This will only become so when we understand how the unity of the structure of care is achieved through temporality. Such an accomplishment will be the object of our discussion in the following and final part.

Time and History

Heidegger makes it clear that the whole of chapter three of division two is a repetition of the analytic of Dasein, but now through the analysis of time (BT: 352). I do not think it is necessary, for our explanation, to go through the argument in the extraordinary detail that he does, but merely to capture the essence of what is being discussed (in fact, the last three chapters are almost a summary of the whole of the argument of *Being and Time*). As we noted at the end of the last part, what is of primary concern to us here is how Heidegger re-interprets the structure of Dasein's Being in terms of time. Unlike our previous exposition, we shall make no attempt to explain each section, but only follow the central themes as they move from one section to the next and across the chapters. It is certainly the case that none of this analysis should surprise us, since Heidegger has already, throughout *Being and Time*, spoken of the three parts of the structure of care (facticity, existence and fallenness) by way of time. He does so now, however, explicitly.

What is significant to them all is the difference between existential time (we might say 'lived time', as long as this is not misunderstood as a series of experiences) and clock or calendar time. The former is the ontological basis of the latter, and the relation between the future, present and past in existential time is quite different from our common sense conception of time which Heidegger describes in the last chapter. Between the first and last chapters, Heidegger applies existential time to a specific problem: how do we exist historically? The answer to this question demonstrates more vividly how Dasein exists temporally, and why this should be not confused with the metaphysical conception of time as a series of now points arising one after the other. The order of Heidegger's argument is as follows: scientific time has its basis in our ordinary experience of time which has its source in the Being of Dasein. Our exposition follows this order and this part is divided into three sections: 'Inauthentic Temporality', 'Authentic Temporality' and 'History'. The presentation of the argument in *Being and Time*, however, is the other way around and begins with the temporality of Dasein. This is because the overall aim of the work is to show that the Being of Dasein is the clue to the meaning of Being in general. We have turned the order around because it better agrees with the phenomenological explanation which must begin with our everyday experience and then the birth of our metaphysical and scientific image of time from there.[53]

Inauthentic Temporality

Possibly if someone were to ask us about time, we would think that it was some kind of mysterious physical substance (in the same way that we might think of space), that things were in and that this substance could be measured by instruments. And we might even believe we would understand the nature of time better the more accurate these instruments were. Yet, Time is not a property of things (like colour) but a way of Being. It is not an adjective but an adverb. We might already have a premonition of this meaning of time in our everyday experience. Do we not feel sometimes that time is moving quickly when we are enjoying ourselves and are interested and very slowly when we are bored, and that this sensation has nothing to do with how fast the hands are moving around the clock (in fact sometimes we can be so bored they seem to moving backwards)? This does not mean time is merely a subjective phenomenon, if we mean by 'subjective' fictional and illusory, since we really do live temporally, but it is not a physical property of the universe existing separately from us. The universe is temporal because we are, and not the other way around.

In the language of *Being and Time*, we can say time is existential rather than categorical. But what does existential time look like? Another common way of looking at time is as a straight line. We think of ourselves now existing in the present, and this present disappears into a past which is no longer, then another now will appear from a future which is not yet, and so on endlessly. The more we think of time as a line, however, the more puzzling it might seem. For if we exist in the present how long is it? Does it not disappear as soon it exists? As soon as we say 'now' it is no longer now and so on. Time then would appear to be nothing, but we do appear to experience the passing of time. The purpose of Heidegger's analysis of time in *Being and Time* is twofold: first, to show that Dasein's Being is temporal, and second, that this temporality cannot be understood through this common sense image of time. Indeed this image of time has its origin in our ordinary experience of time which has its roots in Dasein's temporality. This does not mean that this image of time is false, but it is ontologically derivative. Such an image of time might be useful for scientific experiments, but it is not how we experience time.

Time is not a succession of 'nows', as Heidegger argues in section eighty-one, but this is precisely how philosophers have always attempted to understand it (BT: 472–80). Now this should not surprise us, since the history of philosophy has always covered over the distinctive nature of Dasein's Being, because it has understood Being generally as a substance, as though all Being were the same as the Being of things present-to-hand. Within this history, the most important philosopher is Aristotle, with whom we have already noted Heidegger always has an ambivalent relationship, since Aristotle both opens up, first of all, the question of Being, and, at the same time, closes it down by initiating this metaphysics of substance. The same in the case of time. Aristotle is the most important philosopher of time and determines how it is thought in philosophy right up until Hegel (indeed it is this metaphysics which nourishes the scientific image of time).

Here, turning to the lectures of *The Basic Problems of Phenomenology* can be a very useful supplement to our reading, because Heidegger gives his students a detailed reading of Aristotle's description of time, which is absent from *Being and Time*.[54] It is not necessary for us to follow it in every detail, but a quick overview can show us what is involved in thinking of time as a succession of now points on a line and the problems that might arise. For Aristotle, like his contemporaries, the experience of time is inseparable from motion. Motion does not just mean movement, but also change; and this seems to be what we mean by time when we say something is at t_1 and has changed at t_2. So at eleven o'clock the water was frozen, and thirty minutes later it was liquid because of the heat applied to it. When something changes, we do not think the change is outside it. Rather, it is the changing thing which changes and nothing else. Time, on the other hand, does not belong to the changing thing. It is everywhere, and yet at the same time, Aristotle says, and it is 'alongside' the thing, otherwise how would we be able to say something changes through time? Time cannot be the same as change, as others before Aristotle had believed, but there can be no time without it. The function of time is to count change, just as we used it in our first example: t_1, t_2. t_3, until infinity. Time is just this numbering: 1, 2, 3 . . . Time is not change and change is not time, but we encounter time in change when we count. This counting does not exist in the world, but is an activity of the human soul. It is because we count that we have an experience of time. We can say, 'Now1, now2, now3', and so on, until infinity. Time, then, is just the measurement of change in the broadest sense.

When we come to look, however, at Aristotle's explanation of the experience of time in more detail, more and more problems seem to emerge. Why should we think of time in this way? Heidegger focuses on a particular part of Aristotle's definition, namely that the counting of time takes place within 'the horizon of the earlier and later'.[55] If we imagine time as a line on which we count points, then each point is earlier or later, or before or after, other points on the line. Even t_1 is before the moment of counting, and t_2 is after, and so on. But are not 'before' and 'after', 'earlier' and 'later' temporal terms, and where do they come from? The counting of time seems to be dependent on them, but they themselves have nothing to do with counting. They are experiences of time and not the counting of numbers. This brings us back to the argument of *Being and Time*. The common sense or scientific image of time as a succession of now points is dependent on our everyday experience of time which is not linear at all. It smuggles in this everyday experience without drawing attention to it, constructs an image of time from it, and then explains our everyday experience with the image of time rather than the other way around.

Heidegger's distinctions are very subtle here, so it is worth paying attention to them. He is not saying that the conception of time as a line is false, but it involves an ontological horizon which it leaves in the dark. Such a horizon is our own experience of time. In a limited way, this is already visible in Aristotle's text, when he says the counting of time in relation to change is an activity of the human soul, but his notion of activity is very limited here, and the image equally so. What Heidegger shows is that there is more involved in counting 'nows' than Aristotle makes out. It is not just an experience of number but time. This is because when we experience time we experience a process or a transition. Even in the limited example of change, I do not just count up the changes of place, but experience the movement from one place to the next. If I did not retain the previous place, and expect the next, then I would have no experience of change at all. I can only say 'now there', Heidegger points out, because I retain the previous 'now' and expect the next one. All of this, he adds, I assume when I look at my watch or a clock on the wall, and say, 'Now it is twenty minutes past three.'[56] This appears the give the 'now' more thickness than is initially implied by to limited image of the time line. Every now point both refers to a 'no longer' and a 'not yet'. But what gives this time this dilation and stretch?

Why do we have clocks? Does time matter to us because we have clocks, or do we have clocks because time matters to us? Surely it is the latter and not the former? The only way to find out the meaning of time is through Dasein's involvement in the world. There are not any 'nows' in the universe, rather we measure change through time because it is useful for us. The restricted image of time has its birth place in our more ordinary day-to-day experience of the world. Such an origin is visible in the fact that even this limited image of time has to use the time-determinations 'before' and 'after', 'earlier' and 'later'. There is time because we use time, and the use of time must have origin in the temporality of Dasein. Heidegger's argument here is exactly the same as his displacement of the primacy given to scientific and theoretical reasoning elsewhere in *Being and Time*. Rather than interpreting our pragmatic involvement with things in the world through cognition (present-to-hand), we should interpret cognition through involvement (ready-to-hand). Likewise, rather than understanding time through clocks, we should understand clocks through our use of time.

In *The Basic Problems of Phenomenology*, Heidegger gives a wonderful phenomenological description of clocks and the telling the time, but at this point I want to return to our reading of *Being and Time*.[57] Again we need to remind ourselves that we are reading these chapters backwards. Heidegger's argument is from authentic temporality, to 'world time' or practical time, and then finally to scientific or metaphysical time. We, however, are going the other way, as he does in these later lectures. What, then, in *Being and Time*, does Heidegger say about the derivation of clock time? To answer this question we need to read sections seventy-nine to eighty-one (BT: 458–80). Why do I need to ask you what time it is? Why do I have a clock or watch, or have the time permanently displayed on the taskbar at the bottom of my computer screen?[58] I must have all these ways of telling time, because they serve some kind of purpose or function. Now we have already come across this idea of function before and that is in the description of equipment.[59] Things only have a function because they fit into an activity of Dasein (an 'in order to'), and such activities only have a unity because of the overall significance of the world. If we are to make sense of clock time, therefore, we have to place it within the context of 'world time'.[60]

We tell the time because time matters to us. What Heidegger says is we 'reckon' with time. What he means by 'reckoning' is not the counting that Aristotle describes, but something far more pragmatic. I assign things a time because they are important to me. This time might be movement of the sun across the sky (which is almost paradigmatic for Heidegger: 'The sun dates the time which is interpreted in concern' [BT: 413]), or a change of the seasons or of the hands of a clock, but what matters to me is the assignation. Tomorrow, I have to go to the office, late summer is the time for making hay, there is a meeting at 3 p.m. which I cannot miss. What we notice about all these assignations, which are part of my reckoning with time, is that they all have a certain time no matter how long their duration. Heidegger calls this 'datability' (*Datierbarkeit*). It is this 'datability' which is the true origin of time as a series of nows. I think of each significant assignment of time as a particular 'then' and it is this 'then' which becomes reified into a infinite series of nows. The pragmatic origin of the metaphysical view of time is only visible through the 'before' and 'after' and 'earlier' and 'later'. Being 'now' is not a property of a thing, but a 'making present' or 'enpresenting' (*Gegewärtigen*) in relation to Dasein. If we are to understand the time of things, clocks or calendars, then we can only do so through Dasein's ability to make things present. But this making present can only be made sense of through time as a whole. Making present is significant only in relation to the past and the future as it is experienced by Dasein. So the reason that 'before' and 'after', 'earlier' and 'later' are implicit to time, and every now point is stretched between a 'no longer' and the 'not yet', is not because of a strange property of time as some kind of mysterious substance which things are in, but because the Being of Dasein is temporal. Why, then, do we end up interpreting time as though it were a line of nows? We already know the answer to this question. For the most part, Dasein understands itself through its everyday experience of the world (fallenness). I am so involved with things in the world that I interpret myself as they are rather than what I am. It is this inauthentic temporality which has become the source of our metaphysical image time, which is then reinforced by its legitimation as it passes down through the history of Western philosophy, such that we are now certain that it is the scientific measurement of time which is true and our own experience of time false. This is not a matter, as we have already underlined, of replacing an objective with a subjective viewpoint, but of uncovering the ontological ground which is prior to this distinction and which is Dasein's Being.

Authentic Temporality
Time is not a substance, but a way of Being, and more specifically a way in which Dasein is. I am not in the past, present and future, rather

I am my past, present and future. We have to understand this existential time very differently from categorical time. It is, for example, orientated towards the present, whereas existential time is directed towards the future. We shall see this changes fundamentally how we think about the unity of time itself. As we now know, categorical time has its origin in the experience of everyday time or world time. But it has its basis there in a very particular way. Categorical time is an offshoot of inauthentic existence or fallenness. It is this inauthentic temporality which Heidegger describes in the fourth chapter, 'Temporality and Everydayness' (BT: 383–423). Authentic existence is not the opposite of inauthentic existence, but comes from it. It is, to use Heidegger's language, a modification of inauthentic existence, but in describing authentic existence we see what the ontological roots of both are. We might think of categorical time as the ossification of inauthentic temporality (hardening the present into narrowing of the now), whereas authentic temporality is its dissolving (through the freedom of the future whose ultimate possibility is the nothingness of death). In the former, I lose myself in my absorption in my concern about things, whereas in the latter, I come back to myself through anxiety. What I find there, as we saw from the previous part, is not something, but literally no-thing. It is the 'nothing' which liberates me from the tyranny of things and the stiffening of actuality. Time might be the great destroyer, but what it gives to Dasein is its ultimate freedom and meaning.

How then do I experience the everyday time of care? First of all what matters to me is the present. Not of course as a now point on a line, but in terms of what I am busying myself with. This might be what I am going to do in the next hour, or in twenty years' time, but what is common to them both is that I am taken over by my real or imagined actualities. Rather than my being the source of my life, my life seems to be source of me. I feel trapped and alienated by what I do. My occupations occupy me and my daily life flows along like the famous image of the river of time. In being busy with the present in this sense, the past only appears as something to be retained and finally forgotten when it no longer matters, and the future only expected in relation to what is required and needed. It is this time which holds together the continuity of my everyday world. I expect things to be how I remember them. Everyday life is a ritual glued together by time. This is the real meaning of the transcendence of the world. As we remember from earlier, the world is not a thing in which I am contained like water in a glass.[61] The world is not a being, but the way in which Dasein is. Because Dasein exists temporally, then the world too is temporal. The world is a form of time, its consistency and familiarity.

But just as my life can be lived as fallen, and for the most part it is, where all that concerns me disappears into idle talk, curiosity and ambiguity, and time is just the next moment disappearing into a past already forgotten and a future yet jaded, then I can also be authentic, which means facing my possibilities as my own. This too must be thought temporally. I can only be these possibilities because there is another way of Being in time. If inauthentic time orientates itself in the present, then authentic temporality is fundamentally directed towards the future.

Such a trajectory is already visible in Dasein's own existence. Heidegger defines existence, as we know, as possibility.[62] I am my possibilities. A stone is what it is, but I am what I am not. Not through a simple negation or destruction, but because I can project myself ahead of myself. Such a projection is not a simple plan or project, for this is the future of inauthentic time: merely waiting or expecting something in relation to what I decide or want. As Mulhall writes, projection is not an activity, but something I am.[63] I do not decide to be in the future, rather I am my future. This is what is disclosed to me in my understanding. It is the future which makes the possible possible, not the possible the future. If Dasein were not already in the future, then there could be no possibilities. I, like the stone, would be just carried along by time outside of it.

We know from our reading of *Being and Time* that Dasein does not just exist through its understanding but also in its moods.[64] How does Dasein live through its moods temporally? Moods are what reveal my world as the past. In German, 'I have been' is '*Ich bin gewesen*', literally, 'I am been'. The past is not something which has gone and is lost forever in the next moment, rather I am my past. The past is something which lives through me and in which I live. Just as what is possible is only so through the future, then facticity and thrownness (the fact that I exist already in a world which precedes me) is only made possible by the past. Without the past the world could not weigh upon me. Temporally, then, moods belong to the past.[65]

I can be in a mood inauthentically or authentically, and the two illustrations Heidegger uses here are already familiar to us: fear and anxiety (BT: 389–96). From initial viewing, fear would seem to be a poor example to illustrate the pastness of moods, since am I not afraid of what comes to me from out of the future? But what is it exactly that I fear when I am afraid of something? I fear for myself and more precisely the world in which I already live. I fear the flood because it will wash away this world, the world I have been thrown into and not some future one. Such a fear does not, however, reveal the pastness of the world, even though it springs from it, because I am so occupied with the present that I cannot see it. All that matters to me, quite naturally, is saving my own possessions, my wardrobe as it floats past my window. It is anxiety, on the contrary, that reveals to me the totality of my existence, but it only does so by separating me from the present of my concern.

Only with anxiety can we see for the first time what an authentic, as opposed to an inauthentic, temporality might be. In inauthentic time, it is the present or 'making present' which is central, and the past and the future are orientated towards this endeavour (the metaphysical and scientific image of time as a succession of now points is a pale reflection of this ordinary everyday time). In authentic temporality, on the contrary, it is the future towards which the unity of time is directed. I live my past and my present through the future, rather than my past and future through the present. This gives a completely different flow to existence. It means the past is not something which was and the future just what will be (a 'no longer' and a 'not yet'), but what I come to be through the future (or it comes towards me out of the future) and this future past is what I experience in the present. This present, which is the result of this movement of the 'future past', is quite different from the present of inauthentic time. Heidegger, borrowing this phrase from Kierkegaard, in order to distinguish it from the inauthentic present of keeping busy calls it, a 'moment of vision' (*Augenblick*) (BT: 387). If in everyday concern, I lose myself in the flow of time, then in this 'moment of vision' (which comes to me through anxiety), I am thrown back upon myself. This is why authenticity is not an empty projection into the future, but always determined by our past. We come to our past authentically as a possibility of our future and we take up what we already were. Such an authentic relation to the past, Heidegger calls 'repetition', as opposed to the inauthentic relation, which he calls 'forgetting'.

We have now seen that the structure of care is temporal. Existence is the future, facticity is the past, and fallenness is the present. We have also seen that time can be temporalised in two ways: authentically and inauthentically. In the first, the present is primary, and in the second, the future. Yet, as Heidegger has already said at the beginning of division two, it is not enough just to describe what Dasein is from the outside, but we have to ask ourselves if it is possible for Dasein to be like this at all. Such an attestation is only given through Being-towards-death (BT: 274–8). Our final question in this section, therefore, has to be what is the relation between death and time?

To answer this question we have to go back to where Heidegger begins, chapter three: 'Dasein's Authentic Potentiality-for-Being-a-Whole, and Temporality as the Ontological Meaning of Care' (BT: 349–82). At the beginning of this chapter, Heidegger asks himself whether he has only arbitrarily stuck resoluteness and Being-towards-death together. Why should death be the ultimate future through which all my other futures must be weighed? Cannot it be that I could be equally resolute about other possibilities? No, because the future possibility of death is very different from all other possibilities and so only it can call me to be resolute. It is for this very reason that I shy away from it and busy myself with the world. It is death, in other words, which allows me to make the distinction between authentic and inauthentic temporality, between future which is mine and the future which belongs to everyone indifferently.

The future possibility of my death differs from any other possibility because it reveals my life as a whole, rather than just parts of it. Whenever I am occupied with something, it fills my attention. I lose myself when I am involved and absorbed in the world. When, however, I am anxious of my death, then my whole life is visible to me in a moment. I ask myself, 'Why I am doing this? 'How did I get into this situation?' I am not asking about this or that activity or occupation, but the significance of my life as a whole. These are very different questions. In the first, I identify myself with partial realities, my profession, status or role in life. In the second, I see all these are substitutes for the ultimate meaning. Not that this question tells me what I ought to do (it is precisely this kind of moralising Heidegger avoids). On the contrary, it shows me I am nothing and not identifiable with any of these. It is only because I am not so that I can choose authentically to individually have a profession, status or role. It is only the future possibility of death which shocks me into this insight, because as a possibility it is the possibility of my impossibility. Only this future is mine, because no one can die my death for me. All my other futures could be someone else's. Whatever I do, someone could equally do in my place. When Heidegger writes that Dasein 'shatters' itself against death it is not a celebration of morbidity, but the freeing of my possibilities (BT: 437). For the first time I own what I have become in all its finitude.

Only through the anticipation of my future death can I choose myself. Thus resoluteness and anticipation are not wilfully pushed together, but the first is part of the second. If you face your death as yours, then you will choose your existence individually rather than have it chosen for you by the They. But why is this future more future than any other? Being towards death is only authentic if I relate to my death as a possibility and not as an actuality. It is not my future as something which will happen at a definite time (something I can always, therefore, put off), but an indefinite future. Being-towards-death is a permanent possibility of my life, not an actuality which ends it. It is upon this indefinite future that all my definite futures are projected, and it shows them all as inherently fragile and insubstantial. This is the real truth of human finitude. Not that we are not God, or even that God is dead, but our existence is without solid ground. We are ciphers you and I, and our masks only hide the nothingness beneath them.

History

If Dasein is essential futural, this does mean its history is of no interest to it, but we do have to think of it in a different way. To some degree this chapter ('Temporality and Historicality') is itself a historical curiosity, and Heidegger (unlike the rest of *Being and Time*) is involved in a local quarrel which we ourselves might not be aware of (BT: 424–55).[66] None the less, I do think it gives us some idea of the practical application of authentic temporality to a specific problem. What are we doing when we do history? Are there historical facts? Can history be treated as a science? Is there even anything objective about history, or is it only a story we tell ourselves?

It should not astonish us by now that Heidegger is going to dismiss out of hand that history is a science. But this does not mean it is merely 'subjective', if you understand by this untrue and relative. On the contrary, if we understand history ontologically, then it is more true than any objective science, because it expresses the way Dasein is. Science comes out of our history. It does not fall from the skies like the meteors which it observes. What does it mean, then, to think about history ontologically? First of all, we have to reject the naive idea that history is just about events which have happened in the past. For why would these events be any more significant than any other? This is not deny these events have happened (no more than it is to deny that the sun would exist if the human race were to end), but they only have a significance because they mean something for us now.

Heidegger's approach, as always, is phenomenological. He asks us (in section seventy-three) to think about an object in a museum (BT: 429–34). What makes this object something which belongs to the past? Is it a property like redness or hardness? But anything that I could say about something past, I could also say about something I am using now. Even if I say it is worn down and broken, then there are things in the present which are too. No, the reason I experience this tool in the museum as something which belongs to the past is because it was part of a world which is no longer present. It belongs to Ancient Greece, for example, because such a world existed. Now the world, as we know, is not an objective property of things, but their ontological condition. Things have a meaning because they belong to a world. The world is their general significance. Such significance has its origin in the Being of Dasein. It is only because Dasein is a being which can have a world that there is a world in the first place and that this world is historical. I do not have a past, because I exist in history, but there is history because I have a past.

But why is the past world of the tool I now see lying in the museum of any importance to me? Only because the past belongs to me in the present. If we are to understand history properly, that is to say, ontologically, then we have to understand it through the temporality of Dascin. We have already seen that the past is not just a 'no longer' in which every present now disappears as soon as it comes out of the 'not yet' of the future. I am my past as my present. But this means I can be my history authentically, just as I can the rest of my existence. From this it follows that my history must be understood in terms of my future. Why do I go into the museum to look at tools of the Ancient Greeks? Because such a understanding belongs to my future projection. Of course, I can go into the museum just to pass the time or because I think this is what educated people should do, yet I can also go there to understand myself, and this is the authentic root of any history. Facts matter because they matter to us in our self-understanding and not just because they have happened. It is perfectly conceivable that at some future date the history of the Ancient Greeks will not matter, but not to those who take the Western tradition seriously, since as Heidegger will show in his writing after *Being and Time*, their decisions have been fateful to our own.[67]

There are two possible relations to history, which mirrors our own experience of the past. Either it is immediately forgotten as it is consumed, or it is repeated as a future possibility. The ontological basis of history is, therefore, repetition. Not as an actuality (which is why there is always something vaguely comic about re-enactments), but as a future possibility. Looked at from this perspective, the Fall of the Bastille did not just happen once on 14 July 1789, but again and again, and it is these repetitions which make the first event significant, not the other way around. The time of history, therefore, is closer to the festival than clock time. The past belongs to me more than any historical text book or a programme on the television, but if I did not exist in the past in this way and have a sense of my continuity with it (a 'life', as Heidegger would say, stretched between birth and death [BT: 425–7]), then none of this would interest me at all. It is because Dasein is thrown into a world that it is historical (a being which has a past). It is not thrown because it is historical.

Just as much as history can be significant for the individual ('fateful' in Heidegger's language), then it can also be so for a people, race or country. A people can only have a destiny because it repeats its past in an authentic manner; that is, it grasps the future which is pregnant there. At this moment, Heidegger seems to imply there can be authentic community which is not the same as the They. These passages also have an uncomfortable tone after the fact. Who cannot but think of Germany's catastrophe when reading the following about the fate and destiny of a people; and there is no doubt that Heidegger was seduced by the Nazis.

Resoluteness implies handing oneself down by anticipation to 'there' of the moment of vision; and this handing down we call 'fate'. This is also the ground for destiny, by which we understand Dasein's historizing in Being-with-Others. (BT: 438)

Does the tragedy of Heidegger's own politics (a tragedy to himself, as to a whole people, and one which we should never forget) render his ontology meaningless? *Ad hominem* arguments have no place in philosophy. What is at issue is not just the meaning of history, but whether it should be the final judge. What is lacking in *Being and Time* is any ethics. Not ethics as an *ethos*, or a calculative morality (which seem to be the only two ways Heidegger can think ethics), but one in which my existence, and the right to my existence is called into question by the other, who is not merely a means by which I can be authentic. Why should the death of the other be any less significant than my own, and why not perhaps even more so?

Notes

1. In the winter semester of 1929–30, 'The Fundamental Concepts of Metaphysics: World, Finitude, Solitude'.
2. For the importance of Aristotle in the writing of *Being and Time*, see *The Genesis of Heidegger's* Being and Time, pp. 227–308.
3. I shall explain this view of time in the section 'Inauthentic Temporality', pp. 84–9.
4. *A Guide to Heidegger's* Being and Time, p. 16.
5. As Jean Grondin informs us, Heidegger had already discussed the nature of questioning in great detail in his lectures prior to writing *Being and Time* (specifically in *Introduction to Phenomenological Research* and *History of the Concept of Time: Prolegomena* [2005]). See 'Why Reawaken the Question of Being?' in *Heidegger's* Being and Time: *Critical Essays*, pp. 15–31 (Polt 2005). This essay, as a whole, is an excellent explanation of the introduction to *Being and Time*.
6. Heidegger's own examples will only make sense to you if you understand that 'science' in German, *die Wissenschaft*, does not just mean the

98   Heidegger's *Being and Time*

physical sciences, such as biology and chemistry, but all forms of human knowledge, even what we would call the humanities.

7. Except when the science itself is in crisis (Heidegger gives one example amongst others, of Einstein's theory of relativity), when it increasingly has to face ontological questions, but then the scientist has to become a philosopher and it might be said the best scientists are (BT: 30).

8. Let me be clear here that I can perfectly imagine a scientist, who has been so indoctrinated by the scientific method, and has no understanding of philosophy at all, could live her life as though science were the answer to everything, even the meaning of her existence, but still this way of living is not itself scientific.

9. I will describe the overall structure of *Being and Time* at the end of this part, pp. 33–4.

10. I will describe what Heidegger means by falling in the section 'Falling and Anxiety', pp. 68–73.

11. Heidegger's early lectures give us some idea of the importance of religious language to the development of his philosophy. See *The Phenomenology of Religious Life* (2004). The experience of the early Christianity (as opposed to the metaphysics of theology) is also the inspiration of his re-interpretation of time.

12. For Heidegger's own reading of Plato before *Being and Time*, we need to read his lectures *Plato's Sophist* (1997).

13. This is the origin of Derrida's famous method of deconstruction. For his own explanation of the term, see 'Letter to a Japanese Friend' in *Derrida and Difference*, pp. 1–5. For the best commentary on deconstruction, see *The Ethics of Deconstruction* (Critchley 1999).

14. For Heidegger's full-scale treatment of Kant's *Critique*, see *Kant and the Problem of Metaphysics* (1997).

15. I shall explain this shift from the present to the future in 'Authentic Temporality', pp. 89–94.

16. This is not entirely true. He did write a small essay called 'Time and Being', but it is not a replacement of the missing third division of part one. On the contrary, it precisely tells us why it is absent. See, *On Time and Being* (1972).

17. These questions go beyond the scope of a commentary, but are perhaps what Foucault was alluding to at the end of *The Order of Things*.

18. Again Levinas (the most important interrogator of Heidegger's description of human existence), will ask whether the other's existence is not

more important than my own. If this is so, would this not reverse the relation between ethics and ontology, such that ontology would have its source in ethics, and not ethics in ontology? For Levinas' most sustained engagement with *Being and Time*, see *God, Death and Time*.

19. In the lectures of the winter semester 1929–30, Heidegger describes the fundamental mood of our age as one of boredom. See *The Fundamental Concepts of Metaphysics: World, Finitude, Solitude* (1995).

20. Even here, however, we each have to face our death singularly, since no one can die my death for me. I will explain our relation to death in 'Being towards Death', pp. 73–9.

21. It is important to underline that Heidegger is not against science, but scientism. As he remarks at the end of this section, to question the ontological assumptions of science is not to criticise the empirical work of these sciences, as though *Being and Time* were offering an alternative science (BT: 50). This is still the case in his later essays on the scientific world view (which he now calls 'technology'), though what is at stake has become even more pressing. See *The Question Concerning Technology and Other Essays* (1977).

22. In the section 'Existence', pp. 26–30.

23. I think Dreyfus is right to translate *sein-bei* as 'being-at-home' rather than 'being alongside', since 'alongside' still has a sense of spatial relation of things, as one thing being next to another thing. See *Being-in-the-World*, pp. 44–5.

24. Heidegger already introduces the language of care in these chapters, but it is only in chapter six, 'Care as the Being of Dasein' that he addresses it directly. We shall have to wait until then to explain it in more detail. See 'Being-towards-Death', pp. 73–9.

25. As I explained in the introduction, 'Phenomenology in *Being and Time*', pp. 12–16.

26. Unless I become anxious that I am wasting my life, see 'Falling and Anxiety', pp. 68–73.

27. In Heidegger's essay 'The Origin of the Work of Art', it is not the breakdown of equipment which makes the world visible but art. See *Basic Writings*, pp. 147–87.

28. This is why Dreyfus' critique of some of the extraordinary claims of AI and cognitive science is still important today. See *What Computers Still Can't Do: A Critique of Artificial Reason*.

29. Are Van Gogh's images of the stars in *Starry Nights* (1889, Museum of Modern Art, New York) any less true than the pictures of the universe

made by the Hubble space telescope? Even if we say that one is truer than the other, this difference must have its source in ourselves. What we mean by the word 'truth' will be the important focus of section forty-four of *Being and Time*, and indeed the rest of Heidegger's career. I shall discuss truth in detail in 'Truth and Reality', pp. 63–6.

30. Such a de-severance of the world, rather than things in the world, is 'visualised' by Heidegger, in his later essays on technology, as 'enfram-ing', where nature and human beings are reduced to resources to be used up. Such an negative meaning of equipment is only alluded to in *Being and Time*, when for example, Heidegger refers to nature as mater-ial for work: 'The wood is a forest of timber, the mountain a quarry of rock; the river is water-power, the wind is wind "in the sails"' (BT: 100). He does distinguish this nature from landscape which 'enthrals us', but makes little of this distinction. For a good introduction to Heidegger's thought after *Being and Time*, see J. Young's *Heidegger's Later Philosophy*.

31. In his book *Being-in-the-World*.

32. It is remarkable that in Descartes' *Meditations* others appear as automa-tons that I cannot really be sure are human like me. See, *Philosophical Writings of Descartes*, p. 21.

33. See, for example, the important essay, 'The Essence of Truth' which was written just after *Being and Time*. Heidegger in *Basic Writings*, pp. 115–38.

34. This levelling down of possibilities Heidegger calls 'publicness' (*Öffentlichkeit*) (BT: 165), but we might wonder if there is a more positive way of understanding the public world, as for example by his student, Hannah Arendt. See *The Human Condition*.

35. In the section, 'Descartes and Spatiality', pp. 46–51.

36. Heidegger's expression for moods, *Befindlichkeit*, derives from the German expression '*Wie befinden sich Sie?*', which means 'How are you?' or 'How do you feel?' It is perhaps unfortunate that the translators of *Being and Time* translate it as 'state-of-mind', which gives it a far too cog-nitivist flavour (BT: 172). Dreyfus' translation 'affectedness' is perhaps better. See *Being-in-the-World*, pp. 168–83.

37. In the section 'Existence', pp. 26–30.

38. In the Introduction at the opening of the section 'Phenomenology in *Being and Time*', p. 12.

39. This past is historical through and through, as Heidegger describes in the last sentences of the section on the understanding (BT: 194). We

have to wait until the end of *Being and Time* for the complete investigation of history from an ontological perspective. See 'History', pp. 94–6.

40. In the section, 'Mineness', pp. 35–9.

41. *History of the Concept of Time* (1985), pp. 260–1.

42. The structure of this ontological hermeneutics is crucial to Gadamer's *Truth and Method*. Heidegger describes the implications of this hermeneutics on his own project at the end of *Being and Time* (BT: 358–64).

43. This is the point of Wittgenstein's famous story about the lion. See *Philosophical Investigations*, p. 190.

44. In the section 'Falling and Anxiety', pp. 68–73.

45. He is careful to underline that we should not take such a reference to be an example of 'word mysticism' (BT: 262). It is because the word says something about the experience of truth, which is phenomenologically attested, that it is significant and not just because the Greeks used it. He stresses the same point in his earlier lectures on Aristotle given in the winter semester 1921–2. See *Phenomenological Interpretations of Aristotle* (2001), p. 93.

46. I explained the meaning of 'de-severance' in Chapter Two, in the section 'Descartes and Spatiality', pp. 46–51.

47. I am thinking here, of course, of Heidegger's infamous seduction by the Nazi party. Safranski's biography is an excellent guide to what actually did and did not happen at this time in Heidegger's life. See *Martin Heidegger: Between Good and Evil*, pp. 225–47.

48. The importance of nothing to the understanding of Being is further reinforced by Heidegger in a lecture he gave just after the publication of *Being and Time*, 'What is Metaphysics?' See *Basic Writings* (1994), pp. 93–110.

49. Blanchot and Levinas reverse this phrase and speak not of death as the possibility of impossibility, but as the impossibility of possibility. Even in Heidegger's analysis, is there not an avoidance of some of the pain and distress of dying? What is important for him is the existential courage in the face of the possibility of death in which I choose to be who I am, but does not dying also strip me of all my power to do just this? See Blanchot's *The Space of Literature*, pp. 87–108.

50. I explained the meaning of discourse in 'Moods, Understanding and Language', pp. 56–63.

51. I have slightly changed the English translation here so as to be closer to the German: *das (nichtige) Grund-sein einer Nichtigkeit*.

52. This is another place in *Being and Time* where Heidegger dismisses ethics. We might be (like Magda King) a little more suspicious of this manoeuvre, since he appears to understand it as only calculative. See King's *A Guide to Heidegger's* Being and Time, pp. 169–70.

53. Interestingly enough, this is also the order of Heidegger's explanation of time in *The Basic Problems of Phenomenology*, which were lectures that he gave just after the publication of *Being and Time* in 1927. These lectures are the most important commentary on this part of the book and should be read alongside it. See *The Basic Problems of Phenomenology* (1982), pp. 227–330.

54. *The Basic Problems of Phenomenology*, pp. 231–56.

55. Ibid. p. 240.

56. Ibid. p. 245.

57. Ibid. pp. 257–61. He also discusses clock time in the *Zollikon Seminars*, which is a good introduction to this thought, because here he is speaking to psychiatrists rather than philosophers, and therefore expects no prior knowledge or expertise. See *Zollikon Seminars* (2001), pp. 28–80.

58. Notice that this is a very different question from Aristotle's. We are asking not, 'What is time?', but, 'Why is there time?' Questions involving a 'what' tend to make us think we are talking about some kind of substance, and it is precisely this way of thinking about time that Heidegger is trying to move us away from.

59. In 'World', pp. 39–46.

60. What Heidegger means by 'world time' is not a time common to the world (such as Greenwich Mean Time) but the time belonging to Being-in-the-world.

61. In the section, 'World', pp. 39–46.

62. As I described in the section 'Existence', pp. 26–30.

63. *Routledge Philosophical Guidebook to Heidegger and* Being and Time, p. 149.

64. As I described in 'Moods, Understanding and Language', pp. 56–63.

65. An excellent literary example here would be Proust's *In Search of Lost Time*, when the narrator bites into the madeleine and conjures up the past of his childhood (p. 47ff.) Is this not exactly what Heidegger means by a mood revealing the world to us? It does so always temporally through the past.

66. For an informative summary of this context, see Barash's essay 'Historical Meaning in the Fundamental Ontology of *Being and Time*', in *Heidegger's* Being and Time: *Critical Essays* (Polt 2005), pp. 169–88.

67. I am thinking here of Heidegger's discussion of technology and its origin in Ancient Greek thought. The importance of the history of philosophy to philosophy follows from Heidegger's conception of Being of Dasein. We cannot dismiss the past out of hand because it makes us what we are in the present, see *The Question Concerning Technology and Other Essays* (1977).

3. Study Aids

Glossary

Ability-to-be/potentiality for Being (*Seinkönnen*)
A phrase which turns up often in *Being and Time* and which describes Dasein's Being as an accomplishment or achievement. To be human is not merely a description of a state of affairs like describing what it is to be a stone, but something one does. This is because the fundamental character of human existence is the difference between authenticity and inauthenticity. I can either be myself, or not. What robs me of my ability to be myself is the They and what gives me back the ability to do so is death. On the whole my ability to be is obscured from me by my occupation in the everyday world. I am so busy with things and people that I never face up to who I am, but even these undertakings have their basis in my ability to be. The fundamental ontological condition of my ability to be is temporality, which is why time is a clue to the meaning of Being in general.

Ambiguity (*Zweideutigkeit*)
Part of the threefold structure of falling, the other two being idle chatter and curiosity. It could be mistaken for an inauthentic mood, since idle chatter is a corollary of discourse and curiosity of understanding. Rather than being a mood, however, ambiguity is a confusion specific to interpretation. Because everything has become endlessly fascinating in idle chatter and curiosity, I now no longer know what is important or not. I am bemused by the world.

Anticipation (*Vorlaufen*)
Literally in German, it means 'running ahead' and describes my relation to death as a possibility. Heidegger distinguishes it from expectation, as a particular kind of projection of the understanding. When I
expect something, I imagine its realisation, but anticipation is the
holding onto its possibility. Thus, in Being-towards-death, I anticipate
my death as a permanent possibility, rather than expecting it as something which occurs at the end of my life (which I usually imagine as
some time in the future). In such an anticipation, whose condition is
the call of conscience, I resolutely face up to my own ability to be.
Resoluteness, therefore, is always an anticipation of my death, and
Heidegger will combine the two as anticipatory resoluteness.
Anticipation also highlights the fact that the temporality of authenticity is future orientated, as opposed to the temporality of inauthenticity which is directed towards the present.

Anxiety (*Angst*)
It is of great importance to understand anxiety to make sense of the
distinctive nature of the Being of Dasein. One of the most important
tasks of *Being and Time* is to show that Dasein is not the same as a thing.
No doubt, it can be investigated as a thing (this is what a scientist does),
but this does not exhaust its ontological meaning. What is most distinctive about Dasein is that its Being is an issue for it. This is what
Heidegger means when he says Dasein always has an understanding
of Being. He does not mean by this that it has a definition or concept
of Being always ready to hand (like the definition 'rational animal').
Rather, it exists through this understanding. In my everyday existence,
this understanding is, on the whole, not revealed to me. I am too busy
with the affairs of the world. This is why anxiety is so important to the
argument of *Being and Time*. Moods reveal to me the state of my world
(what Heidegger calls 'facticity'), but the peculiarity of anxiety is that
it does not reveal, unlike fear, a particular state of the world, but my
world in general. In so doing, it illuminates, if only momentarily, the
source of the world in the Being of Dasein. Because it reveals the
world in general and not specifically, then equally, the ontological
origin of the world cannot be a specific possibility of Dasein, but the
Being possible as such. In relation to the transformation of the possible into the actual, then, Being possible is nothing, and this is why I

recoil from it in horror. What anxiety reveals is that at its heart Dasein is nothing, which in Being-towards-death Heidegger will describe as the 'possibility of impossibility'. It is through and in this nothingness that I have resolutely to grasp my Being and authentically choose who I already am. Where I was, I must be.

Assertion (*Aussage*)
Heidegger's word for judgement, as in the proposition, 'The hammer is heavy'. For Heidegger, propositions are derivative of interpretation, which in turn, is based upon the understanding.

Authentic/Inauthentic (*Eigentlich / Uneigentlich*)
The difference between the authentic and the inauthentic is not a moral but an ontological one. The key to understanding their meaning is the German. *Eigentlich* derives from *eigen* meaning 'own'. I can either own my existence or disown it. If I own my existence, then I make it my own by resolutely choosing my possibility to be. The opposite, disowned existence, is one in which, rather than choosing my possibilities, I let others choose them for me. I follow the crowd. For the most part my existence is inauthentic. I live by rituals and habits of thought. Authentic existence comes out of inauthentic existence and is made possible through anxiety in the face of the possibility of my death.

Being/being (*Sein / Seiendes*)
There is something faintly absurd about explaining such a distinction in a glossary, when it was the aim of Heidegger's whole philosophical life. Very crudely, Being refers to how things are, and being to a specific something. You might think of Being as verbal and being as nominal. This explains the tautological expressions which you find in *Being and Time*, such as 'world worlds'. The ontological explanation of Dasein, therefore, concerns how Dasein is, as opposed for example, how a stone, plant or animal is (to use a rather traditional ontological hierarchy). Such an ontological investigation should be sharply distinguished from an ontic one which only describes what something is and not how it is. Because in English (unlike German), the difference between these two notions of being is not obvious, many translators and commentators capitalise the verbal sense of being to distinguish

it from its nominal sense. Others, however, think this capitalisation leads to a mistaken belief that Being is some kind of mysterious higher substance (by analogy with the word 'God'). In this case, the difference between Being and being can only be provided by the context of the passage.

Care (*Sorge*)

The structure of Dasein's existence is care which has three elements: Being ahead of itself, Being already in the world, and Being alongside beings encountered within the world. Being ahead of itself is projection and understanding, Being already in the world is facticity and thrownness, and Being alongside beings encountered in the world is falling. There are also two modes of care: concern, which is the pragmatic relation to beings as ready-to-hand, of which the present-to-hand is a further modification; and solicitude, which is the relation to others. Finally, each element of the structure of care has its ontological basis in temporality. Being ahead of itself is the future, Being already in the world is the past, and Being alongside beings encountered in the world is the present.

Categorical (*kategorisch*)

Being and Time describes two ways of Being, the categorical and the existential. The categorical way of Being belongs to those beings which Dasein encounters in the world. It is the way of Being which has been the basis of ontology since Aristotle and which *Being and Time* overturns. Dasein ends up describing itself as categorical because it is so absorbed in these beings through fallenness that it thinks of itself in the same way.

Concern (*Besorgen*)

One form of care (distinguished from solicitude) where Dasein relates to beings in the world. Heidegger gives the following as examples of concern: 'having to do with something, producing something, attending to something and looking after it, making use of something, giving something up and letting it go, undertaking, accomplishing, evincing, interrogating, considering, discussing, determining . . .' (BT: 83). Concern, as an activity of Dasein must be distinguished from any kind of theoretical or cognitive attitude. In being concerned with things, I am absorbed and involved. They are ready-to-hand as opposed to present-to-hand.

Conscience, Call of (*Ruf des Gewissens*)
The description of Being-towards-death explains what it means to be authentic Dasein, but it does not tell us how any individual can accomplish it as an existentiell. If in my everyday existence, I lose myself in the They, how do I win myself back? To face up to my death as a possibility, have I not already had to have broken with them? Such is the call of conscience which comes from within Dasein. It is the unsettling voice which questions everything I have achieved and accomplished. Unlike the idle chatter of the They, it does not say anything at all, but is the silent ontological disquiet disclosed to me in anxiety. It is the voice of conscience which calls me to be resolute in anticipating the possibility of my death, and in so doing choosing to be myself authentically. I can only do so by recognising my guilt. The style of this language is theological or religious, but its content is ontological. It is a description of what it means to be human and stands or falls on this basis.

Curiosity (*Neugier*)
One of the three elements of falling, the other two being idle chatter and ambiguity. It is an inauthentic corollary of the understanding. Rather than taking a stand upon my existence and owning my possibilities, I simply run from one to the other because everyone else does. Here, everything is endlessly new and novel, but nothing is of any significance or importance.

Dasein
Heidegger's word for human existence which is usually left untranslated. Like much of his supposedly technical vocabulary, it is an ordinary German word meaning existence and specifically human existence. Equally, however, as is also usually the case, we need to be aware of its etymology. Literally translated *Dasein* means 'being there'. The reason why Heidegger avoids expressions like 'human existence' or 'human beings' is they can imply that *Being and Time* is an ontic investigation, attempting to define what it means to be human in the way that the other social sciences do. Dasein is an ontological term, which describes the way in which human beings are rather than what

they are. More specifically, the etymology suggests we should think of the Being of human beings as disclosure.

Datability (*Datierbarkeit*)

Part of our common experience of time. Time is not first of all a series of now points on a time line, but a chain of significant events. This evening I am going out to the restaurant. Tomorrow, I will be meeting my friend. I always have lunch at 1 p.m. and so on. It is because events are significant for us that we have clocks and calendars, and not the other way around. Such events are part of the structure of care which has its ultimate source in authentic temporality.

Death/Being-towards-Death (*Sein-zum-Tode*)

It is not death as the end of life which interests Heidegger (a fact which is not specific to Dasein anyway), but my relation to death in my life. In the first case death is an actuality, something that happens to me and other beings (including the universe, if the laws of thermodynamics are correct), whereas in Being-towards-death, it is a possibility. As a possibility, death is something which can happen to me at any time. I cannot avoid it and have to face up to it myself. In so doing, it forces me to confront the meaning of my life as a whole. Thus, in the anxiety in the face of the possibility of my death, my Being becomes an issue for me for the first time. Facing up to this possibility is what Heidegger calls resoluteness and without it I would not be able to be authentic. Equally, running away from the possibility of my death, and occupying myself with the business of the world, is the origin of the inauthentic.

De-severance (*Ent-fernung*)

The distance and direction of Dasein's spatiality is not geometrical but lived. In being concerned about things I bring them closer and by doing so I take their distance away from them (which is the literal meaning of the German). Such a space is not something which is measured but is part of my existence. What is close geometrically (like the glasses on the end of my nose) could be furthest away existentially.

Destruction (*Destruktion*)

The name of the method by which Heidegger reads the past history of Western philosophy. This method has two different strategies, one which is positive and the other negative. The negative strategy is to demonstrate how this history has distorted the meaning of Being; and the positive, how such a meaning can also be retrieved from the margins of the same history. It is an important precursor of Derrida's deconstruction.

Disclosure (*Erschlossenheit*)
Fundamental to the meaning of Dasein and truth. Truth is not first of all a property of propositions or statements, but a way in which Dasein relates to beings in the world. Only to the extent that Dasein makes them present do they have any truth at all. This 'making present' Heidegger calls disclosure. Such an illumination and manifestation of beings is inseparable from the 'there' of Dasein which is the literal meaning of the German *da*. It is for this reason that Dasein is not a nominal definition of something (like 'rational animal') but an onto-logical description of a way of Being. Dasein is as Being-there and as Being-there other beings are present and have a meaning. Dasein's Being, therefore is the revelation of the Being of all other beings and thus the origin of the meaning of Being in general which is a presenc-ing. This presencing has a far more complex temporality than the meta-physics of substance describes and it is explained in the second division of *Being and Time* through Dasein's concern with things in the world.

Discourse (*Rede*)
Heidegger is not a philosopher of language (at least at the time of writing *Being and Time*) if we mean by that someone who thinks reality is constituted by words rather than simply represented by them. What matters in discourse is what is said and not the saying itself. This is why authentic discourse can be silent, for it is not the words which are significant but what is communicated, which is a shared world that already has its own intelligibility and significance (already 'articulated' in Heidegger's vocabulary), and so is not dependent on any linguistic expression. Discourse, then, strictly speaking is not language, but an attitude of Dasein. The inauthentic mode of discourse is idle chatter.

Ecstasis (*Ekstase*)
Not to be confused with a mystical state, ecstasis depicts the tempo-rality of Dasein. It describes the way in which Dasein 'stands out' in

time by projecting itself into the future through the past and into the present. Ecstasis, therefore, is the temporal form of the transcendence of Dasein.

Environment (*Umwelt*)

The world closest to us in our everyday existence. The world of making a cup of tea, going to college and driving a car. To get along in this world I do not need to have a direct acquaintance with things or a picture of the world in my head. On the contrary, in this world things are familiar to me. Like every world, its source is the Being of Dasein. Philosophy has tended to ignore this world for the sake of cognition, but Heidegger reverses the relation between them. It is not cognition which is the basis of my ordinary experience, but ordinary experience the basis of cognition.

Epistemology

The study of the nature and legitimacy of knowledge in philosophy. *Being and Time* can be read as an ontological critique of epistemology, which was dominant both in neo-Kantianism and Husserlian phenomenology. I first exist in the world and only then subsequently know it. The primary philosophical question is not 'What do I know?', but 'Who am I?'

Equipment (*Zeug*)

Things which I deal with in the everyday world of the environment. Heidegger uses the example of the hammer which I use to hammer nails into the wood in order to make a shelter for myself. What is important about the nature of equipment is that it does not appear in the same way as things which are described by traditional metaphysics. I do not assign properties or attributes to equipment, rather it is purely functional and in this sense not visible at all. I do not 'see' the door through which I walk every day, I just use it. The Being of equipment is what Heidegger calls the ready-to-hand which he distinguishes from the present-to-hand; the latter being the object of cognition or knowledge. Rather than asserting the primacy of knowledge over use, Heidegger argues it is only because we use things that we need to know what they are.

The Everyday (*Alltäglichkeit*)
Most philosophy, since Plato, attempts to escape the everyday (my daily encounter with things and people in a world) for the realm of eternal ideas and supposedly higher truth. For Heidegger, the only possible route into the question of Being is through the everyday. It has to be the starting point of our investigation, because it already presupposes an understanding of Being, and it is this understanding that Heidegger sets against the metaphysics of substance which has led to the forgetting of Being. What is implicit in my everyday existence has to be made explicit by a phenomenological ontology.

Existence (*Existenz*)
It is important not to understand existence in *Being and Time* through the traditional philosophical distinction between *essentia* and *existentia* (what something is and the fact that something is), but through possibility. Dasein does not just exist in the way that a stone, plant or animal exists; rather it makes its own existence because it is something which matters to it individually. Existence is always something which is mine, whereas *existentia* is merely an indifferent logical statement about all things.

Existentiell/Existential (*existenziell/existenzial*)
Existentiell describes the particular everyday possibilities of individual Dasein, whereas existential represents the ontological structure underlying every unique possibility no matter who chooses it and when it is chosen. What is existentiell, therefore, is specific to a culture, whereas what is existential must be universal. In a more Kantian language, we might say the existential is the transcendental condition of every existentiell. If human beings were not the kind of beings that they are, then they would not have possibilities in the way they do. Stones do not have possibilities because of the kind of being they are. *Being and Time*, therefore, is an existential analysis of existentiells.

Facticity (*Faktizität*)
It does not mean factual in the sense of $2 + 2 = 4$, but describes the way in which our existence is always determined to some extent by our past. The fact that I speak English rather than Japanese, can be an astronaut but not an Aztec warrior, for example, is all part of fac-

ticity. The ontological basis of facticity is thrownness, whose temporal horizon is the past.

Falling or Fallenness (*Verfallen*)
The third element of the structure of Dasein's existence; the other two being thrownness and projection. It is essential to the Being of Dasein that it is always involved and occupied with beings in the world. I am always busy with or doing something. It is for this reason that falling or fallenness should not be understood theologically or morally. It is not a sin Dasein is so occupied and habituated. It is what it is. Falling, however, is the everyday condition for Dasein's own self-misunderstanding of its Being. It is so entangled with the things it busies itself with that it ends up interpreting its own Being as though it were the same as the Being of things. The origin of the metaphysics of substance, which culminates in the forgetting of the question of Being with which *Being and Time* begins, is ordinary experience. Just as the other two elements, thrownness and projection, falling has its specific temporality which is the present, or making present.

Fear (*Furcht*)
One of the two moods which Heidegger describes in any detail. The other is anxiety, from which it is to be distinguished. Fear is ontic; whereas anxiety is ontological (this is why Heidegger calls the latter a 'fundamental mood'). It is ontic because it concerns my attitude towards beings in the world (the lion threatens me, so I fear it), whereas anxiety is ontological because it is my very Being which is at issue.

Guilt (*Schuld*)
In Being guilty, I recognise my existence is always in debt. Not to this or that person or thing, or even God, but to Being itself. I am in debt to my Being, because my existence is thrown. I exist in a world which is not my own creation. What is possible for me is already given in advance, what Heidegger calls facticity. Ontologically speaking, therefore, Being guilty has no moral or theological meaning for Heidegger. It does not mean I owe something ontically, but my existence, as mine, owes something to the past. This does not mean I am determined by the past causally. History is not a collection of facts,

but a future possibility which I can be. Being a student of philosophy is something given as a possibility through a tradition I have been born into, but it is up to me whether I choose it as future possibility. Such a choice is only authentic when I choose it on the basis of my own nullity. What guilt reveals to me is that at the heart of my existence there is nothing but possibility, which is covered over by my involvement and absorption in the everyday world.

Hermeneutics

This has its origin in German theology as a particular way of reading Scripture. Indeed, Heidegger's example for a hermeneutical interpretation in *Being and Time* is a textual one (BT: 192). It is the recognition that every interpretation must always presuppose some meaning in advance and never comes across as something empty of significance. This applies equally to the interpretation that *Being and Time* accomplishes. Heidegger describes it as a hermeneutical ontology, because it must already presuppose what it seeks to describe. Rather than seeing this as a 'vicious circle', we have to understand that the only possible route to Being is through a being which has an understanding of Being. The task of *Being and Time*, therefore, is to make this 'pre-ontological' understanding explicit. It is both negative and positive. Negative, because this pre-ontological understanding is overlaid by the tradition which needs to be 'deconstructed' before we can begin the investigation; and positive, because we have to be able to appeal phenomenologically to this pre-ontological understanding otherwise we would have no measure by which to grasp the meaning of Being. To claim this is a 'vicious circle' is to apply an ontic rule to ontological investigation. That we already exist in a pre-ontological understanding of Being is not an error on our part, but just what it means for us to be at all.

History (*Geschichte*)

The past is not just a collection of dates and facts but part of what it means to be me. History in this fundamental sense Heidegger calls 'historicality'. It is because we are beings which already exist in a past as part of a present that we are historical and not the other way around. Authentic history is more concerned with the future than it is with the past. The past is of importance because it is a future possibility and not dead and gone. History is, therefore, repetition and more than merely the retrieval of lost information.

Idle Chatter (*Gerede*)
The fallen form of discourse where, rather than what is spoken about being important, it is the activity of speaking and the words themselves. The modern world is full of noise perhaps, but is it any more significant for that? Idle chatter is linked to curiosity and ambiguity to make up the tripartite structure of falling. The more curious I am about things, rather than being directly engaged by them, the more I talk; and the more I talk, the less certain I am about what is or is not important.

Intentionality
A specific theory of consciousness central to phenomenology. Any kind of consciousness (thinking, judging, wishing and so on) is always a 'consciousness of . . .'. In other words, I cannot think, unless I think of something judge unless I judge something, wish unless I wish something and so on. *Being and Time* can be seen as a critique of Husserl's overtly theoretical version of intentionality. My first relation to the world is not one of consciousness but concern, which has its own specific concrete directionality. Heidegger's specific critique of intentionality can be found in the *History of the Concept of Time* (1985).

Interpretation (*Auslegung*)
I interpret the world before I make judgement about it. To interpret something means to understand its function. The hammer is for hammering in nails in order to make the house which shelters me from the weather. The ultimate 'in order to' is Dasein's existence. For this reason interpretation has its ultimate source in the understanding. Interpretation is not cognitive. It is more like a practical 'know how'.

Mineness (*Jemeinigkeit*)
This designates a particular way in which Dasein can be distinguished from any other kind of being. We should not confuse this with any kind of solipsism. Mineness does not mean I live alone; rather my existence is always an issue for me in a way it cannot be for any other being. Fundamentally my existence is an issue for me in Being-towards-death, since this is one possibility I have to face myself. Dasein is always

individuated, even when it loses itself in the They. However much I flee from the question of my life, it is still my life I am fleeing from.

Moment of Vision (*Augenblick*)
One of the few phrases in *Being and Time* borrowed from another writer (in this case Kierkegaard). The moment of vision is the authentic, as opposed to the inauthentic, present of care, where, on the contrary, I am absorbed and involved in beings such that my own Being is no longer an issue for me. Through anxiety, where my own nullity is made visible for me for the first time, my present comes to me from the future and I seize my possibilities as my own.

Nullity (*Nichtigkeit*)
Possibly the most difficult idea of *Being and Time*. What is revealed in the ontological interpretation of Dasein is that at the basis of its existence there is nothing. Everything I interpret myself through, my attributes and occupations, for example, are inauthentic because they are not really me (it is this nothingness which anxiety reveals). They are not me, because anyone else could be them. Someone else could have brown hair and grey/blue eyes, someone else could be a philosophy teacher. The only possibility which is truly mine is my death. Not death as a fact, but as Being-towards-Death. In facing this possibility of my impossibility, I see, for the first time, that my existence stands on nothing. My attributes and occupations are merely moments within this nullity. I can be them in two ways: either inauthentically, thinking them as stable and as my real identity; or authentically, as choosing them within this nothingness. If what is at the heart of my Being is a nullity, the possibility of my impossibility, then in choosing to be, I also negate every other possibility. Nullity is what holds Dasein permanently open between possibility and actuality. The ultimate source of the nullity of Dasein is the ontological difference between Being and beings. Being, quite literally, is no-thing. See 'What is Metaphysics' in *Basic Writings* (1994) for Heidegger's further explanation of the relation between nothing and Being.

Ontic (*ontisch*)
An ontic investigation must be distinguished from an ontological one. It concerns the nature of beings as opposed to Being. In other words,

it defines what things are as opposed to how they are. There are many kinds of ontical investigations covering both the human (like history, theology or literature) and natural sciences (physics, chemistry and biology). Every ontical investigation presupposes a ontology which it usually leaves unquestioned. Thus, physics will take it for granted that natural beings are mathematical. For this reason, Heidegger argues ontology has a priority over any ontical investigation. This does not mean an ontology is 'truer' than an ontic study, if you mean by 'truer' has a better grasp of the facts. Ontology does not tell you what something is. It does, however, mean it has a philosophical primacy. Fundamentally for Heidegger, every ontical investigation has its ontological basis in the Being of human beings, and this includes the natural sciences, but the study of what it means to be human is not itself a science.

Ontology (*Ontologie*)
The title that Heidegger gives to the study of Being. It should not be confused with traditional ontology which is the study of beings. The method of *Being and Time* is a phenomenological ontology, a description of the way in which beings are, rather than what they are. Specifically, *Being and Time* is a 'fundamental ontology' (BT: 34). It is the investigation of that ontology that is the basis of all other ontologies. This fundamental ontology is the ontology of human beings (which Heidegger calls Dasein), since Being only has a meaning because we are a kind of being whose Being is an issue for it.

Others, Being-with- (*Andere, Sein-bei-*)
Just as little as I am separate from the world, am I also excluded from others, so that I have to wonder how I know, understand or even relate to them. Being-with-others is part of what it means to be me. This relation belongs to the very way I am. This does not mean I am the same as others or they the same as me. Existence is always individual and singular for Heidegger, but I cannot make sense of myself without others. On the whole *Being and Time* describes mainly the inauthentic relation to others as the They, and only very briefly indicates what an authentic relation to them might be through the positive form of solicitude (and only then from the side of the individual Dasein). There is only one mention of the other relating to me rather

than I to them, and that is the voice of a friend who calls me to be authentic (BT: 206). Even this friend, however, is inside of Dasein (perhaps as a representative of the call of conscience). This lack of a relation to the other as other has been taken by some commentators like Levinas, Blanchot and Derrida, to be one way in which *Being and Time* is part of a bias towards the subject in Western philosophy which even it is not aware of, despite its powerful destruction of the tradition. It is also why Heidegger consistently subordinates ethics to ontology, a practice which continues long after the publication of *Being and Time* (see 'Letter on Humanism' in *Basic Writings* [1994]).

Phenomenology
The philosophical method of *Being and Time* which Heidegger took over from his teacher Husserl. The fundamental basis of this method is the description of phenomena as they are given to us. Heidegger gives a full description of the application of this method in section seven (BT: 49–63).

Possibility/Actuality
The distinction between possibility and actuality is far more important to *Being and Time* than many realise. It has its source in traditional Aristotelian ontology, but whereas this ontology emphasises the actual over the possible, *Being and Time* stresses the possible over the actual. This is because existence is defined as the possible. My existence is not an actuality which can be defined from the outside (even if this actuality is understood as a process – the acorn becoming an oak tree), rather it is a possibility through and through. I am always ahead of myself in the future and always understand myself in these terms. My ultimate possibility is death, but again the existential importance of death is as a possibility and not as an actuality; Being-towards-death and not death as a fact. What is ontologically distinctive about Dasein is that its Being is always a possibility and never an actuality. I am my 'ability to be' (*Seinkönnen*) and not just a collection of actual properties (described from the outside) which go up to make a thing.

Present-to-hand (*Vorhandenheit*)
There are two ways in which things can be for Heidegger (including human beings, if they are treated as things), either present-to-hand or

ready-to-hand. What is present-to-hand is what is given when I look at something. It is the basis of our theoretical grasp of things. Western philosophy takes this to be the primary way in which things are present. The aim of the description of the Being of Dasein, however, is to show that this is not the ordinary way in which we relate to things. Before we ever just look at something, we use it and in use things are never present in this way. In fact they are rarely visible at all. I never see the door I use everyday, unless it does not open because it is broken or locked. This way of Being, where things are used rather than theorised about, Heidegger calls ready-to-hand. Rather than the latter being based on the former, as though I first have to understand things before I can use them, the former is based on the latter. It is because I use things that I might need to understand them. The ontological condition of my relation to things which I use Heidegger calls 'the world', and it in turn has its origin in the Being of Dasein.

Project/Projection (*Entwurf*)
When I say to myself I am going to become a student of philosophy or perhaps one day even teach philosophy at university, then I have a project or projection. Most of my projects are obviously banal, but they are the horizon in which I throw my possibilities forward. Such a push into the future is the basis of my understanding. To have a project for Heidegger is not always to have a well defined plan or intention; rather it describes the way in which Dasein is always ahead of itself in the future no matter what task it is occupied with. In the end, it is the ultimate meaning of transcendence; the fact that at every moment of existence Dasein is always outside of itself. Such an exteriority is eventually to be explained by temporality.

Question (*Frage*)
Philosophy is not about answers but questions. Heidegger's question is Being. Just as important as the meaning of Being is our attitude to it. It is important that *Being and Time* begins with a question and not an answer which it then seeks to prove. This is why it is quite absurd to accuse it of being a failure because it has not answered the question it supposedly it set out with. Heidegger's aim is more modest; not to answer the question of Being, but to reawaken the question within us. This whole notion of philosophy as a questioning is very important in

Heidegger's later writings, and in *Being and Time* he gives a detailed analysis of the structure of questioning itself (BT: 24–8).

Ready-to-hand (*Zuhandenheit*)

The ready-to-hand is to be distinguished from the present-to-hand. It describes the Being of things that I encounter in the everyday world of environment. The emphasis here is on handiness (a meaning which is visible in the German). Something ready-to-hand is present to me through my use of it. It is not visible in the way it might be through cognition.

Reference (sometimes, **Assignment**) (*Verweisung*)

This is way in which within the world as environment what is ready-to-hand is always interrelated. I never encounter something ready-to-hand singly. Rather it is connected to something else which is ready-to-hand. I use the computer towards writing this glossary so that you might better understand *Being and Time* and so on. The ultimate 'in order to' is always Dasein. Things have a function because they ultimately point back to me. The general way in which what is ready-to-hand is interconnected makes up the significance of my world. Significance is not a metaphysical definition of the world but expresses my familiarity with what surrounds me. For the most part, I am not even conscious of it. Only when things do not work as I expect them to might I become concerned with it.

Repetition (*Wiederholung*)

Authentic past as opposed to the inauthentic past of concern. The past is something which I can forget as part of my daily existence, or it can be a future possibility which I repeat. Such a past is not experienced through the present as something which passes away always but constitutes it as a future goal. Past as repetition is fundamental to understanding Heidegger's notion of history and we must hear it when he speaks of the necessary repetition of the question of Being. The authentic past is ahead of and not behind me, vanishing into the distance.

Resoluteness (*Entschlossenheit*)

The German self consciously refers to disclosure (*Erschlossenheit*). Being resolute is a particular way in which Dasein understands its own Being where it faces up to its own ability to be in anticipating its own death as a possibility. It is, therefore, the existentiell condition of authenticity.

Science

Being and Time does not treat the nature of science directly though it is implicit throughout that it cannot answer the fundamental question of Being. Generally, we might see this as a distancing from neo-Kantianism, which saw science and particularly epistemology as the primary task of philosophy. For Heidegger, science can never answer the questions of philosophy, because it is always an ontic rather than an ontological inquiry. For this reason, its own ontological basis is left in the dark. The ontology of the natural sciences has its source in Western metaphysics, and more especially Descartes (which is one reason why *Being and Time* has a long section on Descartes [BT: 122–48].) The aim of *Being and Time* is to replace this natural ontology with fundamental ontology, the description of Being of nature with the Being of human beings. The former has its source in the latter and not the other way around. There is a brief discussion of what it would mean to be an authentic scientist at the end of *Being and Time*, but Heidegger never seems to take this topic up afterwards (BT: 408–18). In his later writings, he is more concerned with how science is taken to be the ultimate truth of beings and what this says about our desire to dominate and control nature (see the essay, 'The Question Concerning Technology' in *Basic Writings* [1994]). It is important to realise this is not a critique of science per se, but 'scientism', the belief (and it is a belief) that science is the only answer to any question.

Serviceability (*Dienlichkeit*)

This is part of the structure of reference or assignment. Things have a use (are ready-to-hand) because they have a function or purpose. This function or purpose ultimately goes back to Dasein. A hammer is a hammer because there is hammering, and there is hammering because there is a use for it. If something does not have a use then it is just a thing and not a tool. A thing is present-to-hand either because it has become an object of theoretical knowledge, or it has no use at all. A hammer on a desert island, where there was no wood, would just be a hammer in this sense, unless of course I had another use for it.

Significance (*Bedeutsamkeit*)
This is the way in which the interrelation of what is ready-to-hand makes up the familiarity of the world which becomes the background of my activity (the way we might talk about a Japanese world or an English one, for example). The world is not a thing or a mysterious substance in which things are placed, rather it has its origin in the understanding of Dasein which understands itself through its possibilities passed down to it from its own history and which it projects ahead of itself into the future.

Situation (*Situation*)
One of those words in *Being and Time* used by Heidegger in his lectures before its publication which are then dropped into the work as though everyone used them. Situation has a precise meaning in *Being and Time* and should not be confused with its ordinary use. To be in a situation for Heidegger is to see the possibilities visible there and to choose them authentically. We are not authentic because we are in a situation, but there are situations because we are authentic. The opposite of situation, therefore, might be ritual or habit which is the usual way that we exist in the world.

Solicitude (*Fürsorge*)
This is the other kind of care, as opposed to concern. It relates to my relation to others. It has a positive and negative form. Negatively, on the whole I am indifferent to the presence of others. Positively, I either try and take them over and dominate them, or I attempt to free them for their own possibilities. Possibly the closest Heidegger gets to any kind of ethics in *Being and Time*.

State-of-mind (**Affectedness**) (*Befindlichkeit*)
This is one way in which the world is disclosed to Dasein. It is not cognition but moods which reveal to me the totality of my world. Moods are not merely subjective phenomena which can be contrasted unfavourably with the objectivity of knowledge. On the contrary, they have a much more powerful ontological revealing power of my Being

than any proposition or statement. In *Being and Time*, Heidegger gives a phenomenological description of two moods: fear and anxiety. The first is ontic and the second ontological. The mood of anxiety is fundamental to *Being and Time*, because it shows how it is possible that Dasein's Being can be an issue for it, and therefore, it can escape the domination and the influence of the They. Many commentators prefer the translation 'affectedness' to 'state-of-mind', because the latter is too cognitive.

Temporality (*Zeitlichkeit*)
Although time is the major theme of *Being and Time*, it does not appear until the last half of the second division. Heidegger distinguishes between many different kinds of time in *Being and Time*. There is the scientific image of time as clock time, which has its origin in the ordinary experience of time as 'world time'. Both have their source in the temporality of Dasein, which Heidegger labels with the German *Zeitlichkeit* so as to distinguish it from the temporality of Being in general, where he uses the German *Temporalität*, and which was intended to be the topic of the third division of part two, but was never written. The general argument of *Being and Time* is to show that the image of time we have as a line (past, present and future) has its origin in existential time which has to be described very differently. Time is not a succession of now points, but the unity of the structure of care. It is not a measurement of change, but the expression of Dasein's Being. Such existential temporality, as opposed to categorical time, Heidegger describes as 'ecstatic'. Dasein literally stands outside of itself in time. I project myself through the understanding into the future, am thrown into the world through the past, and engage with beings in the present. Temporality is not something which measures me from the outside, rather I am time. I accomplish my future, past and present. What is first, ontologically speaking, is not clock or calendar time, but lived time. Equally the direction of time does not begin with the present, but from the future. Dasein, Heidegger says, is essential 'futural' (BT: 372–3). This is because authentic Dasein anticipates its own death (the German for 'future' is *Zukunft*, which means literally 'to come'). Inauthentically, on the other hand, time temporalises itself from the present, and in this way it is the origin of the scientific or metaphysical image of time as a succession of now points.

The They (*Das Man*)
In concern, Dasein is involved with things and others. For the most part I am utterly indifferent to the presence of others in my life. I catch the bus every morning but am hardly aware of who is driving it. The non-conspicuousness of others is related to invisibility of things generally in the ready-to-hand. Others, however, can affect my existence negatively and positively. Positively I can show concern for others (solicitude), where I can either take them over or let them be free to make their own decisions. Negatively, however, others can also dominate my possibilities, but they do so in an anonymous way. I end up thinking and doing what everyone else thinks and does, but if someone were to ask me who was the origin of these ideas and behaviour I would not know. This anonymous effect of others, Heidegger calls the They. Most of my life I live as They do (I am myself really a 'they-self'), but through anxiety and the call of conscience, where I face up to my death, I can live my possibilities as my own even though they might be exactly the same as theirs. Since the They is part of the structure of the care as fallenness (the others being existence and facticity), it should not be understood pejoratively.

Thrownness (*Geworfenheit*)
This is one of the fundamental elements of Dasein's existence (the others being understanding [projection] and falling). Thrownness is the basis of facticity. My Being is not a fact like the existence of a stone. Rather, the fact that I am there, and what this fact involves, is due to me being thrown into a world which has existed before me. The language I speak, the way that I understand myself, the possibilities I can choose to be, are all given to me in advance. The past, therefore, is not something which exists inertly outside of my present, but affects it through and through. This does not mean I am determined by past in a causal fashion. The possibilities given to me are still something I can choose. I have to become my past, or what I was. Thrownness cannot be understood without the projection of the understanding, or understanding without thrownness. Both belong to the temporality of Dasein.

Transcendence (*Transcendenz*)
There are two notions of transcendence in *Being and Time*. One is the traditional definition of Being transcending both species and genus

(I can say everything is, but there is no specific difference which points to the meaning of Being), which has its origin in Aristotle and is repeated in Scholasticism (though in this case it is attached to the definition of God). The other is the transcendence of Dasein. Heidegger replaces the older form with this idea of transcendence. If Dasein is transcendent, then this does not mean it is God. *Being and Time* is the description of human finitude and all this entails, and not a theological treatise, even if it might use religious language. The transcendence of Dasein should be taken literally to mean it is always outside of itself (it is close to the notion of transcendence we find in Husserl's definition of intentionality where consciousness is always defined as 'consciousness of . . .'). It is ultimately related to the idea of existence as ecstatic. Dasein always transcends itself because it always projects itself forward into the future, and through this future experiences its past and present. Transcendence should be understood temporally and not categorically as part of a metaphysics of substance. It is the transcendence of Dasein which is the ultimate clue for the meaning of the transcendence of Being, and not the definition of species and genus.

Truth (*Wahrheit*)
Truth, first of all, is not propositional but a disclosure. If beings were not revealed to me then I could not speak about them. In *Being and Time*, Heidegger uses the example of the crooked picture on the wall. If I do not turn around and look at the picture, then I cannot know whether the statement 'The picture is crooked' is true or not (BT: 260–1). The notion of truth as presence or disclosure is much older than logical truth (which Heidegger is not denying, but only claiming cannot be primary). He points to the Ancient Greek word for truth *aletheia*, which he translates as 'unconcealment'. Truth, rather than just a description of propositions and how they relate to the world, is the activity of bringing things out of darkness into the light (it is therefore closely related to Heidegger's definition of phenomenology). Dasein itself can either exist in the truth or not. This does not mean that it is omniscient, but it can either conceal or disclose phenomena, including itself.

Understanding (*Verstehen*)
Dasein as existence always understands itself through possibilities. Heidegger's definition of understanding should not be confused with

its traditional definition (in Kant, for example) as comprehension or knowledge. Understanding is not to have a plan, scheme or design, in the sense of moving from one co-ordinate to the next, but to exist. It is therefore ontological and not ontic. It has to do with the Being of Dasein and not with a specific state of affairs. Dasein always exists with a pre-ontological understanding of itself, because its Being is always an issue for it. For the most part, however, it exists inauthentically in its concern for things and solicitude for others. Only in anxiety, where it has to face its ultimate facticity and thrownness, does it authentically understand itself as nullity. Every understanding is a projection into the future, but such a future can merely be expecting the next thing that comes along, or anticipating my death, and thereby resolutely choosing myself.

World (*Welt*)
The world is not a container in which Dasein finds itself alongside other beings. Rather, it belongs to the Being of Dasein. What it means to be Dasein is to have a world, and such a world is an accomplishment or activity. It is not a noun but a verb. *Being and Time* is concerned with the ontological significance of having a world in general (what Heidegger calls 'worldhood') and not what it means to exist in this or that culture. In other words, the world is not culture as opposed to nature, but the ontological condition of the distinction between them. For the most part, my existence in a world is inauthentic. I simply occupy myself with things and people in my daily affairs. Only anxiety can reveal to me the general significance of my world as a whole which is fundamentally based upon my thrown projection.

Further Reading

Being and Time is one of those books which it is impossible to understand without reading additional material, and perhaps this is true of every great philosophical work, because they are attempting to make us think about the world and ourselves in a new way, so we need all the help we can get. This is not a full bibliography but a selection of books you might find useful if you need to write an essay or just want to find out more about Heidegger. It is divided into three parts:

Heidegger's own work; commentaries on Heidegger (each with a description of why you might find them useful); and finally the details of other works I have quoted in this book but which are not directly relevant to reading *Being and Time*.

Works by Heidegger
Heidegger, M. (2002), *On Time and Being*, trans. J. Stambaugh, Chicago: Chicago University Press.

One of the key issues of reading *Being and Time* is why it ends without finishing what it has set out to do from the start. The description of the meaning of the Being of Dasein was meant only to be a clue for the question of the meaning of Being in general. We find out that this clue is temporality, but how we are to understand it is left entirely dark except for a few cursory remarks in the last pages. Overall, *Being and Time* was divided into two parts and the first part was meant to have three divisions. What we have, however, is only part one and the first two divisions. The second part was intended to be a 'destruction' of Descartes, Kant and Aristotle through the new ontology of *Being and Time*, and I think we can safely say that Heidegger did achieve this through lectures and other works published afterwards; but the third division, if it had been written, would have developed the meaning of Being in general from the analytic of Dasein. Can we say that *Being and Time* is therefore a failure because it is unfinished? I do not think so, unless we have a very restricted understanding of philosophy. It is not about answering questions, but making us question in a more profound way, and Heidegger always saw his own thought as such a continual questioning. The essay 'Time and Being' in this book explains in some way why Heidegger himself never wrote this missing division. It is not, as much as his later writing is, an easy read, but it does explain some of Heidegger's own unease with his methodology and why his thought had moved elsewhere. This is sometimes described as the famous 'turn' (*Kehre*) in his philosophy from the Being of Dasein to Being as such. It is not we who determine Being, but Being us. This change is also described by Heidegger in 'Letter on Humanism' which can be found in *Basic Writings*.

Heidegger, M. (1977), *The Question Concerning Technology and Other Essays*, trans. W. Lovitt, New York: Harper and Row.

The essays on technology found in this collection again demonstrate the transformation of Heidegger's thought from *Being and Time*. There is little mention of the domination of technology in the modern world there, which becomes the basis of much of Heidegger's later thought, though there are clues of it in the description of Dasein's 'deseverance'. Technology, broadly speaking, can be understood as the abolition of distance and the reduction of all beings (including human beings) to resources to be manipulated and used up. The possibility of an alternative relation to beings is not really visible in *Being and Time*, because of its emphasis on the pragmatic aspects of Dasein's environment. The world is a workshop in *Being and Time*, and except for a brief mention of the 'nature which "stirs and strives" ', there is never a landscape or open country (though we might want to add even this nature is now a resource) (BT: 100).

Heidegger, M. (1982), *The Basic Problems of Phenomenology*, trans. A. Hofstadter, Bloomington and Indianapolis: Indiana University Press.

One of the indispensable lecture series given by Heidegger just around the publication of *Being and Time* (this one was taught in the summer of 1927, so it could not have been closer). I think it is arguable that these lectures are the best commentaries and should always be read alongside the major work. Heidegger was a superb teacher, as many of his students bear witness, and a great communicator of ideas. Not for him the mechanical summary of what others have thought and the reduction of philosophy to learnt material, but a real living and dynamic thinking. He came to his ideas through teaching and working with his students, which is perhaps why many of them became great philosophers themselves. This lecture series is primarily concerned not with the definition of phenomenology as the title might suggest (many of Heidegger's lecture titles are a bit misleading, because he worked out his thought in his lectures and sometimes never got to the topic itself; or he just ran out of time since it took so long to set out what needed to be thought and what lay in people's way to prevent them from doing so). The first part of the course is a 'destruction' of traditional ontology, especially in Kant and its origins in Scholasticism. It could be said to be a portion, therefore, of the second part of *Being and Time*, which was intended to be a destruction of traditional ontologies. The second half of the course is a re-elaboration of the temporality described in *Being and Time* and must be read alongside these sections. It also gives us a clue as to what division three might have looked like, though this finally became a dead end for Heidegger.

Heidegger, M. (1985), *History of the Concept of Time: Prolegomena*, trans. T. Kisiel, Bloomington and Indianapolis: Indiana University Press.

Another of Heidegger's series of lectures, and this one might be even more important than *The Basic Problems of Phenomenology*. Like the previous lecture series, the title is a slight misrepresentation. Really, it is a preliminary version of *Being and Time* and for this reason it is essential for understanding of the content of the latter. Because it is a lecture series and Heidegger is speaking to his students, we might argue it is a little easier to comprehend than the major work, since he provides more concrete examples and images to explain his concepts. The first part offers a detailed analysis of Husserl phenomenology and subjects it to an 'immanent critique' which is the basis of the redefinition of phenomenology in section seven of *Being and Time*. The second part covers the same material of the first division of this work, and a brief analysis of Being-toward-death. Even if you do not read any of the commentaries on *Being and Time*, you should read this. It profoundly illuminates and explains its overall argument for the renewal of ontology through the description of human existence.

Heidegger, M. (1993), *Basic Writings*, ed. D. Krell, 2nd edn, London: Routledge.

An excellent collection of Heidegger's writings after *Being and Time*, which has now become a classic. If you want to expand your understanding of Heidegger's thought through his own work, then this is the place to begin. It contains all the important essays, such as 'What is Metaphysics?', 'On the Essence of Truth', 'The Origin of the Work of Art', 'Letter on Humanism' and 'The Question concerning Technology', which are relevant to any reading of *Being and Time*, both to supplement and develop your understanding (so for example, 'On the Essence of Truth' deepens and broadens the explanation of truth in *Being and Time*, and 'What is Metaphysics?' is absolutely necessary to understand the importance of the 'nothing' in the description of Dasein's Being). The other essays show how Heidegger's thought changed after *Being and Time*, and are important to read in comparison. Thus the 'Letter on Humanism' offers an important self-criticism of *Being and Time* through the reversal of the priority between Dasein and Being because of the latter's residual subjectivism. Rather than escaping the metaphysics of subjectivity, Heidegger comes to see *Being and Time* as its continuation in a different form. The editor, David Krell, also provides a very good introduction to Heidegger's philosophy as a whole, and specific introductions to each of the essays.

Heidegger, M. (1995), *The Fundamental Concepts of Metaphysics: World, Finitude, Solitude*, trans. W. McNeill and N. Walker, Bloomington and Indianapolis: Indiana University Press.

A lecture series Heidegger gave after the publication of *Being and Time* in 1929–30. It is important for two reasons. Firstly, it offers a detailed description of what it means to exist in a world, which can be added to the description of *Being and Time*. Rather than just examining it from the perspective of Dasein, as Heidegger does in *Being and Time*, he argues why it is only humans who have world and not any other being. Secondly, it provides a complex and fascinating description of moods, which complement the analysis of *Being and Time*, but now the fundamental mood is boredom and not anxiety. Also moods are no longer described through the individual but through a historical perspective. Again, this shift from the individual to history is a future sign of Heidegger's move away from the subjectivism or individualism of *Being and Time*.

Heidegger, M. (1997), *Kant and the Problem of Metaphysics*, 5th edn, trans. R. Taft, Bloomington and Indianapolis: Indiana University Press.

Heidegger's book on Kant was first published in 1929. It could be said to be part of the missing second part of *Being and Time* which was intended to be a 'destruction' of the ontologies of Descartes, Kant and Aristotle. Destruction is both negative and positive. Negative, because it show how these ontologies conceal the original question of

Being, and positive, because they have resources within them (despite the intentions of the authors) to reawaken this question. Heidegger focuses on the role of imagination in Kant's *Critique of Pure Reason*, which has sometimes been overlooked by other readers, and how temporality is fundamental to understanding Kant's ontology. This work also shows how far, in his interpretation of Kant, he differed from the then powerful Neo-Kantianism in Germany, which tended to prioritise epistemological over ontological questions.

Heidegger, M. (1997), *Plato's Sophist*, trans. R. Rojcewicz and A. Schuawer, Bloomington and Indianapolis: Indiana University Press.

A reconstruction of Heidegger's lecture course on Plato and Aristotle given in 1924–5. It is not a guide to the immediate argument of *Being and Time* but part of the long gestation of that book. It is a detailed textual analysis of book VI of Aristotle's *Nicomachean Ethics* and the whole of Plato's *Sophist*. Again this engagement with the Greek tradition makes good the absence of the second part of *Being and Time*. It also makes clear how positively we are to understand the 'destruction' of the history of philosophy. *Being and Time* is not so much written against Greek philosophy but written in its shadow, and this lecture series demonstrates that the question of Being is not an arbitrary one, but central to origins of philosophy. Fundamental to the Greek experience of Being is the concept of truth as 'unconcealedness' (*aletheia*) which is crucial to the re-interpretation of truth in *Being and Time*. This is not for the first time reader, but it does deepen our understanding of the link between Being and truth which is fundamental to *Being and Time* and all of Heidegger's subsequent work.

Heidegger, M. (2001), *Phenomenological Interpretations of Aristotle*, trans. R. Rojcewicz, Bloomington and Indianapolis: Indiana University Press.

One of Heidegger's early lecture series given in the winter of 1921–2. It is interesting to see the origin of some of the key concepts of *Being and Time*, especially the idea of care. The language and exposition, however, are very abstract and complex because Heidegger is struggling to discover a new language in order to express his insights. Much of this vocabulary will be discarded. Perhaps more interesting for the Heidegger scholar rather than the general reader, and not as useful as

The Basic Problems of Phenomenology and the *History of the Concept of Time* in understanding the detail of *Being and Time* itself.

Heidegger, M. (2001), *Zollikon Seminars: Protocols – Conversations – Letters*, ed. M. Boss, trans. F. Mayr and R. Askay, Evanston: Northwestern University Press.

This book is a record of correspondence and conversations between Heidegger and a Swiss psychiatrist Medard Boss, and also a transcript of seminars with the latter's students between 1947 until Heidegger's death. It is a fascinating glimpse into the teaching style of Heidegger. Also, because he is speaking with medical and not philosophy students, he starts the philosophical discussion at the most basic level, though he never simplifies the topics that are being discussed. In these seminars, he comes across as a modern Socrates. In relation to *Being and Time*, the discussions about time are particularly interesting, especially concerning the derivative nature of the scientific image of time, and can be compared fruitfully with the material of the second division.

Heidegger, M. (2004), *The Phenomenology of Religious Life*, trans. M. Fritsch and A. Gosetti-Ferencei, Bloomington and Indianapolis: Indiana University Press.

A early lecture series given by Heidegger in 1920–1. It is divided into three parts: 'Introduction of the Phenomenology of Religion', 'Augustine and Neo-Platonism' and 'The Philosophical Foundations of Mediaeval Mysticism'. The first section is particularly interesting in relation to *Being and Time*. Heidegger is not interested in the philosophy of religion in the traditional sense as the proofs of existence of God, but how early Christians experienced their lives as it is attested in their writings. This language is closer to our own experience than the metaphysical language of philosophy, and explains the use of religious tropes in *Being and Time*, which are stripped of any theological baggage. The material on Augustine is also the seed for the description of 'falling' or 'fallenness' in *Being and Time*.

Heidegger, M. (2005), *Introduction to Phenomenological Research*, trans. D. O. Dahlstrom, Bloomington and Indianapolis: Indiana University Press.

Early lectures which Heidegger gave in the winter semester of 1923–4. They offer a version of Heidegger's re-interpretation of Husserl's phenomenology through his emphasis on the Greek etymology which we find again in section seven of *Being and Time*. Like the lecture series, the *History of the Concept of Time*, it also provides evidence of Heidegger's 'immanent critique' of Husserl's phenomenology as the basis of its re-interpretation as the method of *Being and Time*. What is at issue is Husserl's continuation of a Cartesian world view which prevents him from breaking out of his theoretical prejudices. For this reason, we have to go back to the original Greek experience of the world and see how Descartes' ontology (or lack of it) prevents any fundamental renewal of a concrete phenomenology. What is not questioned in Descartes' famous statement, 'I think, therefore I am', is what exactly 'I am' means and how we are to understand human existence. This lecture series is not as useful for directly understanding the argument of *Being and Time* as the *History of the Concept of Time* and *The Basic Problems of Phenomenology* are, but it does demonstrate how important phenomenology is to Heidegger's thought, even though he needed to break from Husserl's influence. It also shows just how consistent his thought is through these years until the publication of *Being and Time* in 1927, where he keeps coming back to the same issues again and again, especially the importance of the 'destruction' of Descartes and the re-invention of phenomenology.

Recommended Secondary Works on *Being and Time*

Blattner, W. (2006), *Heidegger's Being and Time*, London: Continuum.

A student's guide to *Being and Time*, though in fact it comments only on the first division. It is heavily influenced by Dreyfus' book *Being-in-the-World* and could be said to be a simplified version of it. It is written in a lively and vivid style and uses a lot of illustrative examples to make Heidegger's work more accessible to the student. This is a good introduction to Heidegger's critique of epistemology, but it does leave out a lot of the detail of *Being and Time*. The decision (apart from the analysis of death, conscience and guilt) to ignore most of the second division seems a bit strange when it advertises itself as an introduction to the work as a whole. There are useful study questions at the end of each section which the student and teacher might find useful, though some of them are a bit idiosyncratic, which might be the general judgement of the book as a whole.

Dreyfus, H. L. (1991), *Being-in-the-World: A Commentary on Heidegger's* Being and Time, *Division I*, Cambridge: MIT Press.

An excellent commentary on the first division of *Being and Time*. What is so wonderful about Dreyfus's book is that it is not so much a explanation of Heidegger's great work but a re-formulation. *Being and Time* (unfairly, I think) has a reputation of being a difficult book to read because of its technical language. This work re-invents Heidegger's language to make it accessible to the English reader. The origin of this book are the author's courses on Heidegger's *Being and Time* which he taught for many years at the University of California, Berkeley and it is great example of what a wonderful teacher he must be. Without this book, *Being and Time* can seem to be a hermetic and closed text. With it, its true originality and importance to our re-interpretation of ourselves and our world shines through. Like any great book, it does have it own bias which is towards pragmatism and a debate with certain aspects of analytic philosophy. This means that some of the drama and pathos of Heidegger's writing is missing (which some might say is a good thing). Also there is no commentary (apart from an appendix) on division two. None the less, as a lucid explanation of Being-in-the-world it cannot be excelled.

Gorner, P. (2007), *Heidegger's* Being and Time*: An Introduction*, Cambridge: Cambridge University Press.

The latest commentary on *Being and Time* to be published in a series of text books which are intended to guide the reader through the main classics in the history of philosophy. Out of all the commentaries, this sticks closest to the original text and makes constant reference to the German. It does tend to read, however, more as a summary of Heidegger's thought than an analysis. Rather than addressing each section of *Being and Time*, it divides it into main themes (such as 'Truth' and 'Being-in-the-world) and for this reason it lacks some of the detail and finesse of the other more substantial commentaries. None the less, it is useful in understanding the broad sweep of Heidegger's thought.

King, M. (2001), *A Guide to Heidegger's* Being and Time, ed. J. Llewelyn, New York: State University of New York Press.

This is a new and expanded edition of Magda King's *Heidegger's Philosophy: A Guide to His Basic Thought*, which was one of the best guides to *Being and Time* ever to be published, and we must thank the editor John Llewelyn for republishing it with the addition of her commentary on division two. The first two parts of this book (which are a reproduction of the original work) are a detailed explanation of the first division. King writes in clear and transparent style and has a close engagement with Heidegger's text. Nowhere, however, does she let Heidegger overwhelm her (which he has done to others). The greatest temptation with any writer on Heidegger is to adopt his own style and writerly tics. King, on the contrary, lays her argument out in an orderly and intelligible way. The third part of this commentary, which was unpublished in her lifetime, concerns the second division of *Being and Time*, which is absent in Dreyfus' great commentary, and for that reason it is very useful supplement to his reading. Unlike the other two parts, however, it takes less distance from Heidegger's text, and perhaps because of this it has less explanatory power for the introductory reader (this might be because King could not re-edit them before publication). This is not the most basic introduction to *Being and Time*, but like Dreyfus' commentary it is absolutely essential.

Kisiel, T. (1993), *The Genesis of Heidegger's* Being and Time, Berkeley: University of California Press.

Like many great works in the history of philosophy, *Being and Time* can appear to have descended from the heavens fully formed and without precedent. Kisiel's book demonstrates unquestionably that this is not so. As Heidegger's lectures before *Being and Time* now prove, he had actively been engaged with these ideas for many years. This work is a reconstruction from this additional material of the conceptual genesis of the main themes of *Being and Time*. It sets out the context for this work through Heidegger's relationship with Christianity, phenomenology and the history of ontology (especially the importance of Aristotle to his understanding of Being). The book is not really a commentary on *Being and Time* but a great work of scholarly reconstruction which illuminates every stage of the construction of Heidegger's work both in reality (in terms of the historical detail) and conceptually.

Mulhall, S. (2005), *Routledge Philosophical Guidebook to Heidegger and Being and Time*, 2nd edn, London: Routledge.

One of the best introductory guides to *Being and Time*. It offers a simpler explanation than Dreyfus and King's commentaries and should be read before them. It is a systematic retelling of all the sections of *Being and Time* (both the first and second divisions), and is written in a clear and rigorous way for first-time readers, but does not insult their intelligence. It is also illuminated by practical examples and vivid illustrations which make *Being and Time* a lot more accessible. Like Dreyfus' book, however, it is heavily influenced by Pragmatism and Wittgenstein and ignores completely the French Heideggerians. Out of all the commentaries on this work, however, it offers the best explanation of the second division. Like Dreyfus and King, this book is necessary to any student of *Being and Time*.

Polt, R. (1999), *Heidegger: An Introduction*, London: Routledge.

Although this is an introduction to the whole of Heidegger's thought, most of the book is in fact a commentary on *Being and Time*. Like most of them, it concentrates on the first division, and its style and philosophical inclination is influenced by Dreyfus. This work is written in a very clear style, but also has a real engagement with Heidegger's thought and is supported by excellent scholarship (unlike the other explanations of Heidegger's work, it also makes use of much of the lecture material). It is especially good on explaining the question of Being and the concrete analyses of *Being and Time*. It also situates this work within Heidegger's philosophy as a whole and clarifies how the later philosophy differs from it. Finally, it has a useful selective bibliography (with brief annotations) for any reader who might want to take their investigation of Heidegger to a deeper level.

R. Polt (ed.) (2005), *Heidegger's* Being and Time*: Critical Essays*, Oxford: Rowman and Littlefield Publishers Inc.

An excellent collection of essays on aspects of *Being and Time*, which includes both French and German writers. Not all of these essays are for the student or general reader, but one or two are very useful. Particularly to be recommended are Jean Grondin's essay on the beginning of *Being and Time*, 'Why Reawaken the Question of Being' and Jeffrey Andrew Barash's on history, 'Historical Meaning in the Fundamental Ontology of *Being and Time*'. Again this edition has a useful short bibliography which supplements the one given by the editor in *Heidegger: An Introduction*.

Safranski, R. (1999), *Martin Heidegger: Between Good and Evil*, trans. E. Osers, Cambridge: Harvard University Press.

Not a commentary on *Being and Time*, but the best biography of Heidegger, which situates his life within the development of his thought. It is especially important for its careful and balanced analysis and description of the events surrounding Heidegger's rectorship and joining the Nazi party which has created such scandal within the philosophical community. Such terrible facts should not prevent us from reading *Being and Time*, since being a philosopher does not make one necessarily a good person. We should know the truth of Heidegger's involvement and its implication for his philosophy as a whole.

Other Works Cited

Arendt, H. (1998), *The Human Condition*, intro. M. Canovan, 2nd edn, Chicago: University of Chicago Press.

Blanchot, M. (1982), *The Space of Literature*, trans. A. Smock, Lincoln and London: University of Nebraska Press.

Critchley, S. (1999), *The Ethics of Deconstruction*, 2nd edn, Edinburgh: Edinburgh University Press.

Derrida, J. (1994), 'Letter to a Japanese Friend', in R. Bernasconi and D. Wood (eds), *Derrida and Difference*, Evanston: Northwestern University Press, pp. 1–5.

Descartes, R. (1984), *Philosophical Writings of Descartes*, vol. 2, trans. J. Cottingham, R. Stoothoff and D. Murdoch, Cambridge: Cambridge University Press.

Dreyfus, H. L. (1992), *What Computers Still Can't Do: A Critique of Artificial Reason*, 2nd edn, Cambridge: MIT Press.

Foucault, M. (2001), *The Order of Things*, 2nd edn, London: Routledge.

Gadamer, H.-G. (1979), *Truth and Method*, trans. W. Glen-Doepel, ed. J. Cumming and G. Barden, 2nd edn, London: Sheed and Ward.

Gadamer, H.-G. (1994), 'The Thinker Martin Heidegger', in J. W. Stanley (trans.), D. J. Schmidt (intro.), *Heidegger's Ways*, Albany: State University of New York Press.

Heidegger, M. (1962), *Being and Time*, trans. J. Macquarrie and E. Robinson, Oxford: Basil Blackwell.

Heidegger, M. (1996), *Being and Time*, trans. J. Stambaugh, Albany: State University of New York Press.

Husserl, E. (1982), *Ideas Pertaining to a Pure Phenomenology and to Phenomenological Philosophy: First Book*, trans. F. Kerston, Dordrecht: Kluwer Academic Publishers.

Kant, I. (2003), *Critique of Pure Reason*, trans. N. K. Smith, intro. H. Caygill, 2nd edn, London: Palgrave Macmillan.

Levinas, E. (1998), 'Is Ontology Fundamental?', in M. B. Smith and B. Harshav (trans.), *Entre Nous: Thinking-of-the-Other*, New York: Columbia University Press, pp. 1–11.

Levinas, E. (2000), *God, Death and Time*, trans. B. Bergo, Stanford: Stanford University Press.

Proust, M. (2002), *In Search of Lost Time*, trans. L. Davies, London: Penguin Books Ltd.

Wittgenstein, L. (2001), *Philosophical Investigations*, 3rd edn, Oxford: Blackwell.

Young, J. (2002), *Heidegger's Later Philosophy*, Cambridge: Cambridge University Press.

Writing an Essay on Heidegger's *Being and Time*

For many, the only reason they will encounter *Being and Time* is as part of a university course, and probably the way they will be assessed is through writing an essay. In this part of the student guide, I want to suggest what kind of questions you might be expected to answer, and how you might go about doing so to the best of your ability.

Types of Questions you might Encounter

It is never possible to be totally sure what the specific content of any question could be, but by targeted research on course outlines which are online, and by using a bit of common sense, you can be fairly certain the following types of questions might turn up. If you are lucky your course tutor might suggest how to answer the questions outlined in your course, and if not, why not ask?

1. What Questions. They can be the hardest to answer often because they seem to be the simplest. These kind of questions might take the form of, 'What does Heidegger mean by Being-in-the-World in *Being and Time*?' You can substitute for the phrase 'Being-in-the-world' any concept or notion in the book. They appear easy, because it seems all you have to do is summarise what Heidegger says. But there are two problems with this: firstly, it can be very difficult to discover what Heidegger means; and secondly, even if you think you know what he does mean, it can be very difficult to organise your answer. I will speak in detail below about how to write an essay, but the danger in writing these kinds of questions (which is why they should really be avoided by course tutors) is you can precisely end up just summarising what Heidegger says, or even what some commentator has written, without analysing his argument at all (the reasons why he says what he says). Essays written in this style can end up just being a list of interesting things about Heidegger, but lack any structure or form. If you come across a 'what' question, like the one above, the best course of action is to transform it into a 'why' question. So to use our example, do not say, 'What does Heidegger mean by Being-in-the-world?', but 'Why does Heidegger use the expression Being-in-the-world?' In other words, what is the central problem which Heidegger is directing our attention to by using this formulation? As soon as you translate a question into an issue or problem, then you can begin to structure your essay, which is of utmost importance to its writing.

2. How Questions. These are questions which are addressed to the method of *Being and Time*. So, for example, you might find a question which asks you to explain the importance of phenomenology to the overall work. These questions can also take the form of a comparison, which can either be internal or external to the text. Internally, they might ask you to compare two concepts together, so for example,

'How does Heidegger distinguish the ready from the present-to-hand?' Externally, a 'how' question might ask you to compare Heidegger analysis with another philosopher's. Again, for example, 'How does Heidegger distinguish his own conception of phenomenology from Husserl's?' The aim of answering these questions is the same as above. Be careful of just falling into a list or summary. Think what is the primary problem or issue which is at the heart of the method or comparison (of course, in order to be able to answer this you have to do the research, both primary and secondary). Only when you have discovered this can you even begin to plan your essay and write it. So, for the first example, I might argue what is essential to Heidegger's definition of phenomenology in *Being and Time* is the description of beings as they show themselves (and I would probably link this to his description of truth). For the comparison questions, on the other hand, I might argue what is fundamental to the distinction between ready and present-to-hand is the difference between practice and knowledge. Finally, for the comparison between the two different philosophers, I might propose Heidegger is transforming Husserl's theoretical phenomenology into a concrete one. I am not arguing these are the only ways of answering these questions, but what I would suggest to you is that you need, first of all, to find a way into answering them, and such a path is only possible through formulating an issue, question and problem for yourself.

3. Why Questions. In my opinion, these types of questions are more immediately philosophical, and although unlike 'what questions' might initially appear difficult, they are in fact easier to answer because they usually ask you a specific and direct question from which it is easier to construct and plan an essay, and therefore write it. A 'why' question normally asks for your opinion about a specific part of Heidegger's argument in *Being and Time* or a particular concept. So for example, it might take a form such as this: 'Is Heidegger right to argue truth originally means disclosure?' What I am suggesting to you is that you should reformulate this question into the following form: 'Why does Heidegger argue truth is originally disclosure?' Only when you have understood why Heidegger has argued for something can you even begin to put forward your own opinion as to whether you agree or not. My general advice is that no matter what type of question you are faced with in your course you need to change it into a 'why'

question, so you can begin to think about what you are reading as a problem for yourself. Only then can you read *Being and Time* for yourself rather than just be over-dependent on what Heidegger writes, or worse what others have written. You should always think independently, no matter at what level you are doing philosophy. Of course, it is important to read, because this is the only way you can know what Heidegger might have meant, and commentaries are useful in aiding your own understanding, but what is more important is that you ask yourself, 'What was Heidegger's problem?' In other words, 'Why did he write this?' rather than, 'What did he write?'

How to Write an Essay

As I have already indicated above, the most important part of essay writing is not so much the content but the form. If you do not get the form right, then your reader will not be able to follow or understand your argument, and therefore evidence of your own knowledge will be lost. I shall give you two bits of important and crucial advice to successful essay writing in this section: firstly, what the form of an essay should be; and secondly, how you should use primary and secondary texts to support your argument.

The basic structure of an essay is an introduction, main argument and conclusion and the art of essay writing is knowing the proper function of each.

1. Introduction. The main function of an introduction is to answer the question. It is surprising how many students fail to do this because they mistakenly believe the purpose of an introduction is merely to 'introduce'. If you start your essay by waffling on about general stuff about Heidegger, then it is highly unlikely your essay will have any structure thereafter. An essay without structure is one in which the paragraphs follow without any noticeable order. In other words, you could cut the essay up with scissors and it would not make any difference to the argument at all. If you start straightaway by answering the question, then you should be able to avoid this disaster.

One way of improving your writing is imagining it is a conversation. For a start, it will make it more natural and closer to your own voice, which is always better for the reader, but more importantly it will make your argument more direct. If someone were to ask you a question in the street, would you start wittering on? Would they not expect you to answer the question straightforwardly? Once you have answered the question, the next part of the introduction is to give reasons for your answer; otherwise what you have to say is merely an opinion. Let us say I am answering the question, 'Is Heidegger right to suggest the meaning of Being has been forgotten at the beginning of *Being and Time*?' Following from what I said above, I first of all have to transform this question into a 'why' question (which means nothing less than thinking about it). I have to ask myself, 'Why does Heidegger think the meaning of Being has been forgotten and is he right?' If I reply 'yes', then I have to think of the reasons why I agree. One reason might be that the history of metaphysics has led to the question becoming irrelevant. I would also have to think why this must be so. Is it because this history finds the source of the meaning of Being in things other than Dasein? But why has this happened? Heidegger's answer is we are so occupied and involved with the beings we encounter in the world that we end up interpreting our own Being in terms of theirs and reverse the true ontological order of dependence. It is not we who gain our Being from things, but things from us. Notice, in attempting to answer the question and give reasons for it, I am not making general and vague comments about Heidegger the man or his philosophy, but getting straight to the question, thinking about and answering it concisely and to the point. If you do this from the very beginning, then your essay should almost write itself.

2. The main argument. I say the essay should almost write itself, because the introduction already informs you what the main argument should do: provide evidence for the reason or reasons for your answer you gave in the introduction. The issue here is the quantity and quality of the evidence. A useful analogy here is the courtroom (and they say philosophers make good lawyers). A lawyer defends a client (or prosecutes the offender) by providing evidence for the judge and the jury. Now she does not want to provide evidence which is irrelevant or prolix, otherwise she might bore or confuse her listeners and lose the case. As a general rule it is always quality over quantity. Again those essays which have no form or structure tend to have a lot of information, but it is haphazard and hit or miss. Your aim is to convince a reasonably intelligent audience (and let us hope your marker is one of these!) with enough evidence to convince them that your reasons for

your argument are valid. If we go back to our analogy of the court-room and we imagine I am defending you on a murder charge (unlucky you), then I might provide the court with character witnesses, an alibi, or even show that the blood on your shirt is not that of the murder victim. Hopefully, through this evidence, I convince the jurors and the judge that you could not have committed the crime. It is exactly the same with essay writing. Generally, you need to provide at least three bits of evidence. Less, and I do not think you would convince anyone, more and you might bring in irrelevant material and start to confuse your readers. Of course, this is only general advice; sometimes four items might be required, but you should always be trying to evaluate your evidence rather than just providing as much as possible (this is what markers mean when they distinguish between analysis and summary – to analyse means to evaluate, discriminate, make a judgement). I always have to ask myself what is the best evidence I can provide for my argument and not how much I can do so.

When it comes to essay writing, however, what evidence am I giving? If I am talking about a humanities essay, then it is always textual. The only evidence I have for anything Heidegger has thought is the books he has written. Unfortunately, he is dead so I cannot ask him what he meant (though I do not believe the writer has any better understanding of what she has written than the reader, so even if Heidegger were alive it probably would not make a difference). There is no absolute right or wrong in essay writing, but that does not mean you can say anything at all. I cannot answer our example question above by claiming the forgetting of the question of Being has to do with climate change (an absurd example, I know), because there is no evidence Heidegger wrote about this. In providing my evidence, I have to think of the places in the text which support the reason or reasons I have given for my answer in the introduction. If I am coming to these because I want to provide evidence, then I should be interpreting rather than just summarising them. So, for example, if one of the reasons I do give for the forgetting of Being is the confusion of Dasein's Being with the Being of things, then I might want to look at the sections in *Being and Time* where Heidegger describes the phenomenon of 'falling' or 'fallenness', but always with emphasis on my argument and not just repeating what he says.

Providing material and evidence for an argument is where research comes into the planning of your essay, because if you do not know the text, then you might miss the best evidence for your essay (imagine I was a lawyer and did not know about DNA testing, for example). Our primary evidence is *Being and Time* (it has been translated into two versions, the Macquarrie and Robinson, which I have been using, and the more recent Stambaugh – both are equally good, though of course stick to one or the other). Secondary sources and your lectures and seminars are also excellent guides for the overall structure of the work. There is, however, one other important function of secondary sources and that is to provide additional evidence. Again the useful analogy here is the courtroom. Lawyers always use experts to add weight to their arguments. If I want to prove the blood on your shirt is not that of the victim, then would it not be more convincing to my listeners, if I wheeled on some famous forensic scientist to say this rather than just me? I am a lawyer, what do I know? It is the same with using secondary sources in essays. If in your reading, you can find some famous professor from Yale or Oxford who says exactly the same as you, would that not convince the reader even more that your reasons are valid if you provided this evidence in a footnote or end note? On the whole secondary sources are not part of the main text, unless they are crucial to your argument, but then you have to evaluate the quality of your evidence, as I said above. Also, if you think of secondary sources in this way, then it gives direction to your research, because as soon as you have worked out the structure of your essay, you know what you are looking for, rather than having to read every single word written on Heidegger (an impossibility anyway) or just picking sources randomly from the shelves or the Web. If it is irrelevant, throw it away. You can always read it in another life.

3. Conclusion. Now I am going to be slightly controversial here. I do not think a conclusion is just about concluding, as an introduction is not just about introducing (if you think introducing means waffling on about something and adding a bit of general colour). True you can very quickly summarise your argument, but do not insult your reader, because if you have structured your essay well, then they do not want to read it again. There is nothing more deflating than reading a conclusion which begins with the statement, 'In summary, I have shown . . .', when it is quite clear the writer has not (indeed, why even end the last paragraph with 'In summary . . .', since it is just that?).

Do not think of the conclusion as an ending, but as a chance of saying something new. Psychologically, this will leave your marker in a good frame of mind just before they decide how they are going to grade or mark the essay. But what does 'new' mean here? Just like with the main argument, you have to use your judgement. If you go too far off the beaten track, then you will leave your reader confused, but if you lack ambition, you will end up just repeating yourself, which I am trying to convince you is not such a good idea. There are three ways of expanding the scope of your essay at the end. One is referring to the overall context of text as a whole, since your evidence in the main argument is usually specifically tied to the relevant passages. So in relation to our example question, it might be interesting to point out *Being and Time* does not get around to answering the question of the meaning of Being, because it is only a fragment. Two, I might want to refer to the ambition or scope of Heidegger's philosophy as whole. Again in relation to our question, I might briefly mention his own self criticisms of *Being and Time*, and the change of orientation of his later philosophy from Dasein to Being (again I would have to support this with evidence, as I must do in the main argument of the essay). Three, I could contrast Heidegger's argument with another philosopher, as I have done so in some of the end notes in this book. Is ontology the one and only important question as Levinas suggests? Rather than seeing the conclusion just as the end of your essay, as though it has just run out of steam, view it as setting out new possibilities of research. No essay can answer all of a question, and we must remember even *Being and Time* ends in just this way.

Index

Aletheia, 64
Ambiguity, 69, 91
Anticipation, 79, 94
Anxiety, 70–3, 81, 90, 92
Aristotle, 4, 22–3, 32, 33, 39, 46,
    63, 71, 85–7
Assertion, 61
Assignment, 43–4
Authenticity, 37–9, 67, 71, 73,
    78–9, 83, 90, 91–4, 96

Being, 6–7, 12, 16, 19–25, 27, 33,
    46, 67, 74, 83
Being-with, 54–6

Care, 41, 68, 74, 83, 84, 90,
    93
Categorical, 28–30, 34, 39, 42, 58,
    72, 85, 90
Conscience, 80–1, 82
Consciousness, 5, 8–10
Curiosity, 69, 91

Dasein, 16, 26–7, 35, 36, 39–42,
    45–6, 48–51, 52, 54, 67, 72–3,
    74–5, 81, 95
Datability, 89
Death, 35, 66, 73–9, 93–4

Descartes, 9, 10, 32, 33, 34, 40, 41,
    46–9
De-severance, 50, 69
Destiny, 96–7
Destruction, 29–33, 46
Disclosure, 57, 64–5
Discourse, 62–3, 68, 80
Dreyfus, 1, 51

Environment, 42–6, 60
Equipment, 43–5, 88
Ethics, 2, 97
Everyday, 38–9, 40–1, 44, 69–70,
    72, 82, 90–1
Existence, 27–8, 33, 35, 36, 38, 59,
    91
Existential, 28–30, 34, 39, 42, 72,
    85, 90

Facticity, 58, 81, 91
Falling/fallenness, 29, 70, 75, 89–91
Fear, 72, 92

Guilt, 81–2

History, 31, 94–6
History of the Concept of Time, 6–12, 60
Husserl, 3–8, 10–11, 40, 41

Idle chatter, 68–9, 81, 91
Inauthenticity, 37–9, 67, 70, 89, 92–4
Interpretation, 59–60

Kant, 1, 4, 10, 13, 32, 33, 41, 46, 71
Kierkegaard, 92

Language, 62–3
Levinas, 2
Logic, 60–1, 64

Mineness, 35–8, 53, 71
Moment of vision, 92–3
Moods, 57–9, 69, 91–2
Mulhall, 91

Nothing, 71–3, 81–2, 90, 94

Ontological difference, 47–8
Others, 51, 53–7, 75

Parmenides, 47
Phenomenology, 3–16, 43–4, 95
Plato, 4, 20, 31, 38
Possibility, 35–8, 46, 59, 73, 76–9, 83, 91, 93–4
Present, 32–3, 89, 92

Present-to-hand, 35, 43–4, 46, 47–9, 60–1, 85, 88
Projection, 59, 91, 96

Ready-to-hand, 44, 46, 49, 60–1, 88
Reality, 65–6
Reference, 43–4
Repetition, 93, 96
Resoluteness, 82–3, 93–4

Science, 25–6, 37, 47–50, 88
Serviceability, 45
Signs, 44–5
Situation, 83
Solicitude, 55

The 'they', 53–6, 79–81, 94
The Basic Problems of Phenomenology, 86–8
Thrownness, 58, 91, 96
Time, 32–3, 67–8, 83–94
Truth, 15, 52, 63–5

Understanding, 59–60

World, 5, 8–9, 34–5, 39–42, 44–6, 51, 52, 58–9, 66, 71–3, 81, 87–8, 91, 95